END-USER
Cybersecurity for the Home Office

DEDICATION

This book is dedicated to all home office workers, providing them with the necessary tools to safeguard themselves and their families while navigating the cybersecurity landscape.

We at Cybersnap hope that **"END USER: Cybersecurity for the Home Office"** will equip you with the knowledge and resources to secure your personal and company information against cyber threats.

INTRODUCTION

In the not-so-distant past, the term "office" typically conjured images of bustling workspaces, neatly arranged desks, and the hum of productivity. However, the rapid evolution of technology and the global shift towards remote work have redrawn the boundaries of the modern workplace. Enter the era of the home office—a dynamic realm where kitchen tables double as desks and virtual meetings replace face-to-face interactions. As the world adapts to this new paradigm, an unprecedented challenge emerges on the digital horizon: the imperative need for robust home office cybersecurity.

The digital landscape has become integral to our daily lives, seamlessly intertwining with our professional responsibilities. The boundaries between personal and professional spaces have blurred, creating unique vulnerabilities that demand our immediate attention. "End User" aims to shed light on the paramount importance of cybersecurity in the home office setting and to guide readers through the intricate web of threats that lurk in the virtual shadows.

PUBLISHERS NOTE

Cybersnap is a renowned Cybersecurity organization that was co-founded by Gregory Dharma LePard, its Chief Evangelist and Cybersecurity expert, and Imogen Fannon, Chief Engagement Officer and philanthropy advocate. At Cybersnap, we firmly believe cybersecurity education should be accessible to everyone and presented in a format that all can easily understand. Our mission is to educate and protect you, the reader, as you navigate the ever-changing cyber landscape.

A portion of the proceeds from this book will be donated to **nonprofits that protect against cyberbullying and exploitation.**

This book provides information for general and educational purposes only and is not a substitute for professional advice. Accordingly, we encourage you to consult with the appropriate professionals or do your research before acting based on such information.

First Edition

Table of Contents

DEDICATION 2

INTRODUCTION 3

PUBLISHERS NOTE 4

Chapter 1: Introduction to Home Office Cybersecurity 9

Understanding the Importance of Cybersecurity 9

Recognizing the Risks and Threats in the Home Office
Environment 12

Establishing a Security Mindset 15

Chapter 2: Securing Your Network and Devices...................19

Setting up a Secure Wi-Fi Network 19

Using Strong and Unique Passwords on Wi-Fi.......................22

Using Strong and Unique Passwords in a Home Office..........25

Updating and Patching Your Devices Regularly 27

Tips for Updating and Patching Devices: 28

Chapter 3: Protecting Your Data.......................................31

Backup Strategies and Data Recovery Plans.........................31

Encryption for Sensitive Information.....................................34

Implementing Two-Factor Authentication (2FA) 37

Chapter 4: Safe Internet Practices 40

Recognizing Phishing Attempts and Email Scams..................40

Avoiding Malicious Websites and Downloads 42

Use Virtual Private Networks..45

How to use a VPN in your home office: 46

Chapter 5: Securing Your Home Office Infrastructure 48

Physical Security Measures for Your Workspace 48

Secure Document Management and Disposal 51

Protecting Printed Documents and Sensitive Information 53

Chapter 6: Securing Communications 57

Encrypted Messaging and Voice Calls 57

Securing Video Conferencing and Virtual Meetings 60

Avoiding Social Engineering Attacks 63

Chapter 7: Software and Application Security 67

Managing Software and App Permissions 67

Keeping Software Updated and Secure 70

Keeping Software Updated and Secure at home office 74

Using Antivirus and Anti-malware Solutions 77

Chapter 8: Establishing a Security Policy for Family Members and Guests 81

Secure Access for Guests in Your Home Office 81

Chapter 9: Monitoring and Responding to Security Incidents 85

Detecting Suspicious Activities and Intrusions 85

Creating an Incident Response Plan 88

Reporting Cybersecurity Incidents 92

Chapter 10: Cybersecurity Best Practices for Remote Work 95

Balancing Productivity and Security 95

Using Secure File Sharing and Collaboration Tools 98

Securing Personal Devices Used for Work 101

Chapter 11: Children and Cybersecurity 105

Childproofing Devices and Internet Access 105

Monitoring and Managing Children's Online Activities 108

Educating Children about Online Safety 111

Chapter 12: Privacy and Data Protection 116

Protecting Personal Identifiable Information (PII)..............116

Respecting the Privacy of Others.......................................119

Chapter 13: Secure E-Commerce and Online Transactions123

Safeguarding Online Payments..123

Recognizing E-Commerce Scams and Fraud 126

Tips for Secure Online Shopping..129

Chapter 14: Staying Informed about Cybersecurity Threats
....133

Following Cybersecurity News and Trends 133

Subscribing to Security Alerts and Notifications.................136

Participating in Cybersecurity Communities......................139

Chapter 15: Continuous Improvement and Education 143

Regularly Assessing Your Cybersecurity Measures..............143

Learning from Security Incidents and Mistakes..................146

Encouraging a Cybersecurity Culture at Home 150

Appendix: 154

Security Checklist for Home Office 157

Glossary of Cybersecurity Terms 161

Conclusion 165

ABOUT THE AUTHOR...166

Acknowledgements..167

Our other publications:..168

CHAPTER 1: INTRODUCTION TO HOME OFFICE CYBERSECURITY

Understanding the Importance of Cybersecurity

Cybersecurity is of utmost importance for a home office because it helps protect your digital assets, personal information, and sensitive data from unauthorized access, theft, or damage. As more people work remotely and rely heavily on digital technologies, the risks associated with cyber threats have increased significantly. Here are some key reasons why cybersecurity is crucial for a home office:

1. *Protection against Cyberattacks:* Cybercriminals constantly seek vulnerabilities in computer systems and networks to exploit for their gain. Home offices are often perceived as softer targets compared to corporate environments, making them more susceptible to attacks like phishing, malware, ransomware, and data breaches. Implementing robust cybersecurity measures can help prevent such attacks and reduce the risk of falling victim to cybercriminals.

2. *Safeguarding Personal and Financial Information:* In a home office, you might handle sensitive information like bank details, personal documents, and client data. If this information gets into the wrong hands, it could lead to identity theft, financial loss, or other fraudulent activities.

Cybersecurity measures, such as strong passwords, encryption, and secure data storage, help protect this valuable information from unauthorized access.

3. *Preserving Business Reputation:* A home office data breach or security incident can seriously damage your professional reputation. Clients and partners may lose trust in your ability to protect their data, which can have long-term consequences for your business. By prioritizing cybersecurity, you demonstrate that you take data protection seriously and can be trusted with confidential information.

4. *Ensuring Business Continuity:* A cyber attack can disrupt home office operations, leading to downtime and financial losses. For example, ransomware can lock you out of your systems until you pay a ransom, paralyzing your business. By implementing cybersecurity measures such as regular data backups and secure access controls, you can mitigate the impact of such attacks and ensure business continuity.

5. *Compliance with Legal and Regulatory Requirements:* Depending on the nature of your home-based business and the location, there may be legal and regulatory requirements for data protection and cybersecurity. Failure to comply with these regulations could result in legal penalties and fines. Ensuring your home office is

secure helps you remain compliant with relevant laws and regulations.

6. *Protection of Intellectual Property:* If your home office involves creative work or proprietary information, safeguarding your intellectual property is essential. Cybersecurity measures can prevent unauthorized access to your creative work, designs, or trade secrets, protecting your intellectual property rights.

7. *Mitigating Financial Losses:* Recovering from a cyber attack can be costly, especially if sensitive data is stolen or your systems are severely damaged. Cybersecurity measures act as a preventive investment, potentially saving you from significant financial losses in the long run.

Cybersecurity is vital for a home office because it safeguards your digital assets, personal information, and business reputation. It allows you to work confidently and focus on your professional goals without worrying about potential cyber threats. By staying vigilant and implementing appropriate security measures, you can create a safe and secure digital environment for your home office.

Recognizing the Risks and Threats in the Home Office Environment

Recognizing the risks and threats in the home office environment is essential for implementing effective cybersecurity measures. Here are some common risks and threats you should be aware of:

1. **Phishing Attacks:** Phishing is a deceptive tactic where cybercriminals try to trick you into revealing sensitive information, such as login credentials or personal data. They often use emails, messages, or websites that appear legitimate but are designed to steal your information.

2. **Malware:** Malicious software (malware) includes viruses, Trojans, worms, and ransomware. Malware can infect your computer and cause damage, such as data loss, system crashes, or unauthorized access.

3. **Weak Passwords:** Using weak or reusing passwords across multiple accounts increases the risk of unauthorized access. Cybercriminals can use password-cracking tools or stolen credentials from other breaches to gain access to your accounts.

4. **Unsecured Wi-Fi Networks:** Working from home might involve using public Wi-Fi or poorly secured home networks. Hackers can intercept data on unsecured networks, potentially compromising sensitive information.

5. **Lack of Regular Updates:** Failing to update your operating system, software, and security patches leaves your devices vulnerable to known exploits and vulnerabilities.

6. **Insider Threats:** While less common in home offices, insider threats can still occur. It involves malicious or negligent actions by someone with authorized access to your systems or data.

7. **Physical Security Risks:** Inadequate physical security, such as leaving devices unattended in public spaces, can lead to theft or unauthorized access to sensitive information.

8. **Social Engineering:** Cybercriminals may use social engineering techniques to manipulate or deceive you into divulging confidential information or performing certain actions.

9. **Unauthorized Access:** Allowing others to use your devices or having weak access controls can lead to unauthorized access to your data and systems.

10. **Data Loss and Lack of Backups:** Not having regular data backups can result in permanent data loss in the event of a cyber attack, hardware failure, or accidental deletion.

11. **Internet of Things (IoT) Devices:** Smart devices connected to your home network can become entry points for attackers if not adequately secured.

12. **Third-Party Risks:** If you collaborate with external vendors or use third-party services, their security practices can also impact the security of your home office environment.

To mitigate these risks and threats, consider implementing the following cybersecurity best practices:

- Use strong and unique passwords for all accounts and enable multi-factor authentication (MFA) whenever possible.

- Regularly update your operating system, software, and security applications.

- Be cautious with email attachments and links, especially from unknown sources.

- Secure your Wi-Fi network with a strong password and encryption (WPA2/WPA3).

- Use a virtual private network (VPN) when accessing sensitive information on public Wi-Fi.

- Educate yourself about social engineering tactics and remain vigilant against suspicious requests.

- Enable device encryption to protect data in case of theft or loss.

- Back up your data regularly and store backups securely, preferably offsite or in the cloud.

- Limit access to your devices and accounts only to trusted individuals.

- Consider setting up a separate network for IoT devices and changing default passwords on these devices.

By being aware of the risks and threats present in your home office environment and taking proactive security measures, you can significantly enhance the protection of your digital assets and sensitive information.

Establishing a Security Mindset

Establishing a security mindset for your home office is crucial to ensure that you prioritize cybersecurity and take appropriate measures to protect your digital assets and sensitive information. Here are some steps to help you develop a security-focused mindset:

1. **Educate Yourself:** Stay informed about the latest cybersecurity threats, best practices, and updates. Read articles, attend webinars, and follow reputable sources in the cybersecurity industry. The more you know, the better equipped you'll be to make informed decisions.

2. **Identify Assets and Risks:** Take inventory of all the digital assets and sensitive information in your home office. Understand each asset's potential risks and threats, including data, devices, software, and accounts.

3. **Risk Assessment:** Conduct a risk assessment to identify vulnerabilities and potential weaknesses in

your home office setup. Assess the impact of various security incidents and the likelihood of their occurrence.

4. **Implement Strong Password Practices:** Use unique and strong passwords for all your accounts and devices. Avoid using easily guessable information like birthdays or names. Consider using a password manager to help you manage and generate strong passwords.

5. **Enable Multi-Factor Authentication (MFA):** Enable MFA whenever possible to add an extra layer of security to your accounts. MFA requires users to provide multiple forms of identification before gaining access, making it harder for unauthorized individuals to breach your accounts.

6. **Secure Your Home Network:** Change the default login credentials of your router and use WPA2 or WPA3 encryption for your Wi-Fi network. Regularly update your router's firmware to ensure it has the latest security patches.

7. **Use Secure Connections:** When accessing sensitive information or conducting work-related tasks, use a secure and encrypted connection, such as a VPN, especially when using public Wi-Fi.

8. **Keep Software and Systems Updated:** Regularly update your operating system, software applications, and security software to patch vulnerabilities and protect against known threats.

9. **Backup Your Data Regularly:** Implement a reliable backup strategy to protect your important data. Back up your files regularly and store them securely, preferably in an offsite or cloud storage service.

10. **Stay Vigilant Against Phishing:** Be cautious of unsolicited emails, messages, or phone calls that ask for personal information. Avoid clicking on suspicious links or downloading attachments from unknown sources.

11. **Limit Access and Privileges:** Only grant necessary access and privileges to yourself and other users in your home office. Minimize administrative privileges to reduce the potential impact of security incidents.

12. **Physical Security:** Ensure that physical access to your devices is limited, and never leave your devices unattended in public spaces.

13. **Develop a Security Policy:** Create a clear and concise security policy for your home office. This policy should outline cybersecurity best practices, acceptable use guidelines, and consequences for non-compliance.

14. **Regularly Review and Update Security Measures:** Cybersecurity is an ongoing process. Regularly review and update your security measures as new threats emerge and your home office environment evolves.

By adopting a security mindset and prioritizing cybersecurity, you can significantly reduce the risk of security breaches and protect your home office from potential threats. Remember to be proactive and vigilant in maintaining a secure digital environment.

CHAPTER 2: SECURING YOUR NETWORK AND DEVICES

Setting up a Secure Wi-Fi Network

Setting up a secure Wi-Fi network for your home office is essential to protect your sensitive data and ensure a safe working environment. Here's a step-by-step guide to help you establish a secure Wi-Fi network:

1. **Choose a Strong Network Name (SSID):** Avoid using default or easily recognizable network names. Instead, create a unique SSID that does not reveal personal information or identify your home office.

2. **Use WPA2 or WPA3 Encryption:** Select the latest and most secure encryption protocol available, either WPA2 (Wi-Fi Protected Access 2) or WPA3. These encryption standards encrypt data transmitted between devices and the router, making it more challenging for attackers to intercept and read the data.

3. **Set a Strong Wi-Fi Password:** Create a strong and complex Wi-Fi password that combines uppercase and lowercase letters, numbers, and special characters. Avoid using easily guessable information like your name or address.

4. **Change Default Router Login Credentials:** Most routers have default login credentials. Change the default username and password for your router's administration interface to prevent unauthorized access to your router settings.

5. **Enable the Firewall:** Most modern routers come with built-in firewalls. Ensure that the firewall is enabled to filter incoming and outgoing network traffic, providing an additional layer of protection against unauthorized access.

6. **Disable WPS (Wi-Fi Protected Setup):** WPS can be susceptible to brute-force attacks, allowing unauthorized devices to connect to your network. Disable WPS to enhance security.

7. **Disable Remote Management:** Turn off remote management features on your router to prevent attackers from accessing your router settings from outside your home network.

8. **Firmware Updates:** Regularly check for firmware updates for your router model. Manufacturers release updates to fix security vulnerabilities and improve performance. Apply these updates promptly to keep your router secure.

9. **Guest Network:** If your router supports it, set up a separate guest network for visitors. This will isolate guests from your main network and prevent them from accessing sensitive data.

10. **MAC Address Filtering:** Enable MAC address filtering to control which devices can connect to your Wi-Fi network. Add the MAC addresses of your devices to the allowed list and block any other unrecognized devices.

11. **Use a Strong Wi-Fi Password for Guests:** If you provide your guests with your main Wi-Fi network password, ensure it differs from the one you use for your devices. Change it periodically to maintain security.

12. **Disable SSID Broadcasting:** Consider disabling SSID broadcasting, which hides your Wi-Fi network from the list of available networks. While this is not a foolproof security measure, it adds an extra layer of obscurity.

13. **Physical Router Placement:** Position your router in the center of your home office, away from windows and external walls. This helps reduce signal leakage and makes it harder for outsiders to intercept your Wi-Fi signal.

14. **Log and Monitor Devices:** Enable router logging and regularly monitor the devices connected to your network. This way, you can quickly identify any suspicious activity.

Following these steps, you can establish a secure Wi-Fi network for your home office, reducing the risk of unauthorized access and protecting your sensitive data and digital assets. Remember that maintaining good security practices and staying vigilant are essential for a secure home office environment.

Using Strong and Unique Passwords on Wi-Fi

Setting up a secure Wi-Fi network for your home office is essential to protect your sensitive data and ensure a safe working environment. Here's a step-by-step guide to help you establish a secure Wi-Fi network:

1. **Choose a Strong Network Name (SSID):** Avoid using default or easily recognizable network names. Instead, create a unique SSID that does not reveal personal information or identify your home office.

2. **Use WPA2 or WPA3 Encryption:** Select the latest and most secure encryption protocol available, either WPA2 (Wi-Fi Protected Access 2) or WPA3. These encryption standards encrypt data transmitted between devices and the router, making it more challenging for attackers to intercept and read the data.

3. **Set a Strong Wi-Fi Password:** Create a strong and complex Wi-Fi password that combines uppercase and lowercase letters, numbers, and special characters. Avoid using easily guessable information like your name or address.

4. **Change Default Router Login Credentials:** Most routers have default login credentials. Change the

default username and password for your router's administration interface to prevent unauthorized access to your router settings.

5. **Enable the Firewall:** Most modern routers come with built-in firewalls. Ensure that the firewall is enabled to filter incoming and outgoing network traffic, providing an additional layer of protection against unauthorized access.

6. **Disable WPS (Wi-Fi Protected Setup):** WPS can be susceptible to brute-force attacks, allowing unauthorized devices to connect to your network. Disable WPS to enhance security.

7. **Disable Remote Management:** Turn off remote management features on your router to prevent attackers from accessing your router settings from outside your home network.

8. **Firmware Updates:** Regularly check for firmware updates for your router model. Manufacturers release updates to fix security vulnerabilities and improve performance. Apply these updates promptly to keep your router secure.

9. **Guest Network:** If your router supports it, set up a separate guest network for visitors. This will isolate guests from your main network and prevent them from accessing sensitive data.

10. **MAC Address Filtering:** Enable MAC address filtering to control which devices can connect to your Wi-Fi network. Add the MAC addresses of

your devices to the allowed list and block any other unrecognized devices.

11. **Use a Strong Wi-Fi Password for Guests:** If you provide your guests with your main Wi-Fi network password, ensure it differs from the one you use for your devices. Change it periodically to maintain security.

12. **Disable SSID Broadcasting:** Consider disabling SSID broadcasting, which hides your Wi-Fi network from the list of available networks. While this is not a foolproof security measure, it adds an extra layer of obscurity.

13. **Physical Router Placement:** Position your router in the center of your home office, away from windows and external walls. This helps reduce signal leakage and makes it harder for outsiders to intercept your Wi-Fi signal.

14. **Log and Monitor Devices:** Enable router logging and regularly monitor the devices connected to your network. This way, you can quickly identify any suspicious activity.

Following these steps, you can establish a secure Wi-Fi network for your home office, reducing the risk of unauthorized access and protecting your sensitive data and digital assets. Remember that maintaining good security practices and staying vigilant are essential for maintaining a secure home office environment.

Using Strong and Unique Passwords in a Home Office

Using strong and unique passwords in your home office is critical to maintaining cybersecurity. Passwords are the first defence against unauthorized access to your accounts and sensitive information. Here are some guidelines to help you create and manage strong and unique passwords:

1. **Use Long and Complex Passwords:** Aim for passwords that are at least 12 characters long and include a mix of uppercase letters, lowercase letters, numbers, and special characters. Avoid using easily guessable information like birthdays or common words.

2. **Avoid Common Passwords:** Refrain from using obvious or commonly used passwords such as "password," "123456," or "qwerty." Cybercriminals often use dictionaries and common password lists in their hacking attempts.

3. **Create Passphrases:** Consider using passphrases, which are longer phrases or sentences that are easy for you to remember but difficult for others to guess. For example, "MyHomeOfficeIsSecure2023!" is a strong passphrase. However, note that you should not use this as your password.

4. **Unique Passwords for Each Account:** Never reuse passwords across multiple accounts. If one account gets compromised, it could also lead to other

accounts being breached. Use a different password for each online service.

5. **Use a Password Manager:** A password manager is a secure tool that helps you generate, store, and manage complex passwords for different accounts. It stores your passwords in an encrypted vault, requiring you to remember only one master password.

6. **Enable Multi-Factor Authentication (MFA):** Enable MFA for your online accounts whenever possible. MFA requires users to provide multiple forms of identification before gaining access, adding an extra layer of security to your accounts.

7. **Change Default Passwords:** If you have any devices, routers, or software with default passwords (e.g., default administrator passwords), change them immediately after setup.

8. **Update Passwords Regularly:** Regularly update your passwords, ideally every three to six months. This practice reduces the risk of old passwords being compromised.

9. **Use Password Encryption for Files:** If sensitive files require password protection, use encryption software to secure them. This ensures that even if the files are accessed, their contents remain unreadable without the password.

10. **Educate Family Members or Co-Workers:** If you share your home office with family members or co-

workers, ensure everyone understands the importance of using strong and unique passwords. Encourage them to follow these guidelines as well.

11. **Protect Physical Notes:** If you need to write down passwords on paper, store them securely and discreetly, away from prying eyes. Never leave passwords visible or easily accessible.

12. **Beware of Phishing Attempts:** Be cautious of phishing emails or messages that trick you into revealing your passwords. Legitimate organizations will never ask you for your password via email.

Remember that while strong and unique passwords are essential, they are just one aspect of cybersecurity. Regularly updating your software, using antivirus and antimalware protection, and being cautious about online activities are equally important in maintaining a secure home office environment.

Updating and Patching Your Devices Regularly

Regularly updating and patching your devices is crucial to maintaining a secure home office environment. Software developers release updates and patches to address security vulnerabilities, fix bugs, and improve overall performance. Failing to update your devices promptly can make them susceptible to cyberattacks and compromise sensitive information. Here's why updating and patching is essential and how to do it effectively:

Importance of Updating and Patching:

1. **Security Vulnerabilities:** Hackers actively search for vulnerabilities in software and operating systems. When they discover a vulnerability, they may exploit it to gain unauthorized access or cause harm. Software updates often include security fixes to patch these vulnerabilities.

2. **Data Protection:** Updating your devices helps protect your data from potential breaches. Cybercriminals can exploit unpatched devices to steal sensitive information, such as login credentials, personal data, and financial information.

3. **Malware Protection:** Many updates include improved antivirus and antimalware definitions to defend against the latest threats. Regular updates ensure your devices have the latest protection against malware and viruses.

4. **Stability and Performance:** Updates can improve the stability and performance of your devices, ensuring they run smoothly and efficiently.

5. **Compatibility:** Software updates often include compatibility improvements, ensuring your devices work seamlessly with the latest applications and services.

Tips for Updating and Patching Devices:

1. **Enable Automatic Updates:** Whenever possible, enable automatic updates for your operating system, software applications, and security software. This ensures that your devices receive critical updates as soon as they become available.

2. **Check for Updates Manually:** Regularly check for updates if automatic updates are unavailable or not enabled. Look for updates in the settings or preferences section of your device's operating system or software.

3. **Update All Devices:** Remember to update all devices connected to your home office network, including computers, laptops, smartphones, tablets, routers, and IoT devices.

4. **Backup Your Data:** Back up your important data before performing major updates. Although updates are designed to be seamless, unforeseen issues can occur, and having a recent backup ensures you can recover your data if necessary.

5. **Verify Software Sources:** Only download updates from official sources or reputable app stores. Avoid downloading updates from unfamiliar websites or clicking on links in suspicious emails.

6. **Update Your Router's Firmware:** Routinely check for firmware updates for your router and apply them as needed. Router firmware updates address security vulnerabilities and can enhance the overall performance of your network.

7. **Keep Plugins and Add-ons Updated:** If you use browser plugins or add-ons, keep them updated to ensure they have the latest security features and bug fixes.

8. **Update Connected IoT Devices:** If you have smart devices connected to your home network, such as smart cameras or smart speakers, check for and apply updates for these devices.

By staying proactive about updating and patching your devices, you significantly reduce the risk of falling victim to cyber threats and ensure that your home office remains a secure and protected environment for your work and sensitive data.

CHAPTER 3: PROTECTING YOUR DATA

Backup Strategies and Data Recovery Plans

A robust backup strategy and data recovery plan for your home office is essential to protect your critical data and ensure business continuity in the event of data loss or disasters. Here are some guidelines to help you create effective backup strategies and data recovery plans:

1. Identify Critical Data:

- Determine which data is critical for your home office operations. This may include work documents, financial records, client data, and other information you cannot afford to lose.

2. Choose Backup Solutions:

- Consider using a combination of local and cloud-based backup solutions for redundancy. Local backups (external hard drives, network-attached storage) offer quick access to data, while cloud backups provide offsite storage and protection against physical disasters.

3. Schedule Regular Backups:

- Set up a regular backup schedule to automatically back up your critical data. Daily or weekly backups may be sufficient, depending on the volume of data changes.

4. Test Data Restoration:

- Periodically test your data restoration process to ensure that backups work correctly and you can recover data when needed. It's essential to confirm that your backups are reliable.

5. Use Versioning or Incremental Backups:

- Choose backup methods that allow versioning or incremental backups. Versioning keeps multiple versions of files, while incremental backups only back up changes made since the last backup. These approaches save storage space and provide multiple recovery points.

6. Secure Your Backups:

- Encrypt your backups to protect them from unauthorized access. If using cloud storage, choose reputable providers with strong security measures.

7. Keep Backups Offsite:

- Store at least one copy of your backups offsite, away from your home office. This protects against physical disasters like fires or floods affecting your home.

8. Implement Redundancy:

- Consider using multiple backup devices or services for added redundancy. This ensures that if one backup method fails, you still have other options for data recovery.

9. Protect Against Ransomware:

- Ransomware is a growing threat. Consider using a backup solution that allows for immutable backups, preventing ransomware from encrypting or deleting your backups.

10. Document Your Data Recovery Plan:

- Create a data recovery plan that outlines step-by-step procedures for restoring data in various scenarios, such as data loss, hardware failure, or cybersecurity incidents.

11. Train Employees or Family Members:

- If your home office involves others, train them on backup procedures and data recovery protocols. Ensure they understand the importance of data protection.

12. Review and Update Regularly:

- Regularly review and update your backup strategy and data recovery plan to accommodate changes in your home office setup or data requirements.

Having a comprehensive backup strategy and data recovery plan will give you peace of mind, knowing that your critical data is protected and that you have a clear plan to recover in case of any data loss or disaster.

Encryption for Sensitive Information

Using encryption for sensitive information in your home office is a crucial step to ensure the confidentiality and security of your data. Encryption is a process that converts plaintext data into ciphertext, making it unreadable to unauthorized individuals. Here's how you can effectively implement encryption for sensitive information:

1. Choose Strong Encryption Algorithms:

- Use well-established and strong encryption algorithms, such as AES (Advanced Encryption Standard), to encrypt sensitive data. AES is widely regarded as secure and is commonly used for data encryption.

2. Encrypt Storage Devices:

- Encrypt your storage devices, including internal hard drives, external hard drives, USB flash drives, and any other portable media that contains sensitive information. Modern operating systems provide built-in encryption features (e.g., BitLocker for Windows and FileVault for macOS) to encrypt storage.

3. Use Full-Disk Encryption (FDE):

- Full-disk encryption ensures that all data on your storage device is encrypted, including the operating system and system files. This provides comprehensive protection against unauthorized access.

4. Encrypt Cloud Storage:

- If you use cloud storage services to store sensitive files, choose providers that offer client-side encryption or zero-knowledge encryption. This ensures that your data is encrypted before it leaves your device, and only you have the decryption keys.

5. Encrypt Communication Channels:

- Use encrypted communication channels when transmitting sensitive information over the internet. Use secure protocols like HTTPS for web browsing and SFTP or SCP for file transfers.

6. Implement Email Encryption:

- Use email encryption tools or services when sending sensitive information via email. These tools encrypt the content of your email so that only the intended recipient can decrypt and read it.

7. Secure Messaging Apps:

- If you use messaging apps to communicate sensitive information, opt for end-to-end encryption apps. This means messages are encrypted on the sender's device and decrypted only on the recipient's device.

8. Protect Encryption Keys:

- Safeguard your encryption keys carefully. Strong encryption is useless if the keys fall into the wrong hands. Use strong passwords or passphrase protectors to secure your encryption keys.

9. Use Encrypted Password Managers:

- If you use a password manager to store your login credentials and sensitive data, ensure that the data stored within the password manager is encrypted. Most reputable password managers employ strong encryption methods.

10. Regularly Update Encryption Software:

- Keep your encryption software, operating system, and applications current. Updates often include security enhancements and patches for vulnerabilities.

11. Educate Users on Encryption Practices:

- If others use your home office network or devices, educate them about the importance of encryption and best practices for securing sensitive information.

By implementing encryption for sensitive information in your home office, you can significantly enhance data protection and prevent unauthorized access to your critical data, ensuring a secure working environment. Remember that encryption is just one layer of a comprehensive cybersecurity strategy, so it should be combined with other security measures for optimal protection.

Implementing Two-Factor Authentication (2FA)

Implementing Two-Factor Authentication (2FA) in your home office is an effective way to enhance the security of your online accounts and protect them from unauthorized access. 2FA adds an extra layer of protection by requiring users to provide two different forms of identification before gaining access to an account. This significantly reduces the risk of someone accessing your accounts even if they have your password. Here's how to implement 2FA in your home office:

1. Enable 2FA for Important Accounts:

- Identify the critical online accounts in your home office that hold sensitive information, such as email, banking, cloud storage, and work-related accounts. Enable 2FA on these accounts first.

2. Choose 2FA Methods:

- Most services offer multiple 2FA methods, such as SMS codes, authenticator apps, hardware tokens, or biometric verification. Use an authenticator app (like Google Authenticator or Authy) or hardware tokens (like YubiKey) for enhanced security compared to SMS codes.

3. Set Up 2FA on Accounts:

- Access the account settings of each chosen service and locate the 2FA or security settings. Follow the instructions to set up 2FA with your preferred method.

4. Save Backup Codes:

- Many services provide backup codes if you lose access to your 2FA device. Save these codes securely and keep them in a safe place in case you need them.

5. Configure Recovery Options:

- Some services allow you to set up recovery options, such as backup phone numbers or backup email addresses. Configure these options to regain access to your accounts if you ever lose your 2FA device.

6. Use Mobile Apps or Dedicated Devices:

- Whenever possible, use dedicated devices (like smartphones) to run authenticator apps or hardware tokens. Avoid using 2FA on shared or public devices.

7. Review 2FA Settings Periodically:

- Regularly review your 2FA settings to ensure everything is up-to-date and that you can still access your accounts. If you change or lose your 2FA device, update your settings accordingly.

8. Train Others on 2FA:

- If others share your home office or have access to your accounts, educate them about 2FA and its importance. Encourage them to enable 2FA on their accounts as well.

9. Use App-Specific Passwords:

- Some apps or devices might not directly support 2FA, but they allow you to generate app-specific passwords. Use these passwords instead of your main password for added security.

10. Prioritize Security Over Convenience:

- While 2FA might require an extra step during login, remember that it significantly enhances security. Prioritize security over convenience to protect your sensitive data.

Implementing 2FA in your home office is a simple yet powerful way to strengthen cybersecurity defences. By enabling 2FA on your critical accounts, you add an additional layer of protection that greatly reduces the risk of unauthorized access and potential data breaches.

CHAPTER 4: SAFE INTERNET PRACTICES

Recognizing Phishing Attempts and Email Scams

Recognizing phishing attempts and email scams is crucial, especially when working from a home office. Cybercriminals often take advantage of remote work situations to launch attacks, so it's essential to be vigilant and follow best practices to protect your personal and professional information. Here are some tips to help you identify phishing attempts and email scams:

1. **Check the sender's email address:** Carefully examine the sender's email address. Phishers often use email addresses that mimic legitimate sources but have slight misspellings or unusual domain names. Be cautious of emails from unknown or suspicious-looking addresses.

2. **Verify the sender's identity:** If you receive an email from a familiar sender that seems out of character or asks for sensitive information, contact the sender through a different means (e.g., phone call) to confirm if they sent the email.

3. **Look for spelling and grammar errors:** Phishing emails often contain spelling mistakes, grammatical errors, or awkward phrasing. Legitimate companies usually have well-written and professional communication.

4. **Be cautious of urgent or alarming requests:** Phishers often create a sense of urgency, making you feel like you need to act immediately. They may claim your account is compromised or that you need to verify your information urgently. Take a moment to think before reacting.

5. **Don't click on suspicious links:** Hover your mouse over hyperlinks in emails (without clicking) to see the actual URL. If the link's destination differs from the email's claims, it's likely a phishing attempt. Avoid clicking on such links.

6. **Be wary of email attachments**: Malicious attachments can contain malware. Only open attachments if you expect them and verify the sender's identity first.

7. **Check for generic greetings:** Phishing emails often use generic greetings like "Dear Customer" instead of addressing you by your name. Legitimate emails from reputable sources usually address you personally.

8. **Be cautious of email content requesting personal information:** Legitimate companies won't ask you to provide sensitive data (e.g., passwords, Social Security numbers) via email. Be skeptical of any such requests.

9. **Review the email's design and formatting:** Phishing emails may have poor formatting or inconsistent designs compared to legitimate emails from the same company.

10. **Use security tools:** Enable email filters, spam blockers, and antivirus software to help detect and block phishing emails.

11. **Stay updated on current scams:** Stay informed about recent phishing trends and email scams. Cybersecurity news and official announcements from companies can help you stay vigilant.

12. **Report phishing attempts:** If you receive a phishing email, report it to your IT department and forward the suspicious email to the organization it claims to be from.

Remember, being cautious and skeptical is key to protecting yourself from phishing attempts and email scams while working from a home office. Always verify with the sender through a separate communication channel before taking action if in doubt.

Avoiding Malicious Websites and Downloads

Avoiding malicious websites and downloads is crucial to maintaining a secure home office environment. Malware and malicious websites can compromise sensitive data and lead to various cybersecurity issues. Here are some tips to help you stay safe:

1. **Use reliable security software:** Install reputable antivirus and anti-malware software on your computer. Keep it updated to ensure it can identify and block the latest threats.

2. **Keep your operating system and software up-to-date:** Regularly update your operating system, web browsers, and other software to patch any known vulnerabilities that hackers could exploit.

3. **Be cautious with links:** Avoid clicking on links from unknown sources, especially in emails or messages. Hover your mouse over links to see the destination URL before clicking. If it looks suspicious, don't click on it.

4. **Type URLs directly:** When visiting important websites like banks, official services, or financial platforms, manually type the URLs into the address bar instead of clicking on links in emails or search results.

5. **Use secure websites (HTTPS):** Always look for the "https://" prefix in the URL and the padlock symbol in the browser's address bar before entering sensitive information. Secure websites encrypt data during transmission, making it harder for attackers to intercept.

6. **Be cautious with downloads:** Only download files from trusted sources. Avoid downloading software, files, or attachments from unknown websites or suspicious links.

7. **Enable your firewall:** Ensure your computer's firewall is enabled to provide additional protection against unauthorized access.

8. **Avoid pirated software and content:** Downloading pirated software, movies, music, or other copyrighted content from untrusted sources increases the risk of downloading malware.

9. **Be wary of pop-ups:** Avoid clicking on pop-up ads, especially those that claim your computer is infected or require you to download something to fix an issue. Legitimate software updates usually come from within the application itself or official websites.

10. **Use ad-blockers cautiously:** While ad-blockers can help prevent malicious ads from displaying on websites, be cautious about the ad-blocker extensions you use. Some ad-blockers themselves could be malicious.

11. **Educate yourself and your family:** If you share your home office with family members, educate them about cybersecurity best practices to avoid accidentally downloading malicious content or falling for scams.

12. **Use a separate work environment:** If possible, create a separate user account or environment for work-related tasks, and avoid using it for personal browsing or leisure activities.

Stay safe online requires a combination of security tools, best practices, and a healthy dose of skepticism. Always be vigilant, and if you encounter any suspicious websites or downloads, report them to your IT department or relevant authorities.

Use Virtual Private Networks

Using a Virtual Private Network (VPN) in your home office effectively enhances your online security and privacy. A VPN encrypts your internet connection, making it difficult for cybercriminals, ISPs (Internet Service Providers), or other entities to intercept your data. Here's why and how to use a VPN in your home office:

Benefits of using a VPN:

1. **Enhanced security:** A VPN encrypts your internet traffic, ensuring that sensitive information remains secure and protected from potential threats.

2. **Privacy protection:** With a VPN, your real IP address is hidden, and your online activities become anonymous to your ISP and other online trackers.

3. **Bypass geo-restrictions:** VPNs can help you access content and services that might be restricted or blocked in your region.

4. **Secure remote access:** A VPN provides a secure connection to your company's servers if you need to access your work network or sensitive data remotely.

5. **Protection on public Wi-Fi:** When you connect to public Wi-Fi networks, a VPN shields your data from potential eavesdroppers on the same network.

How to use a VPN in your home office:

1. **Choose a reputable VPN provider:** Research and select a well-known, trusted VPN service that offers strong encryption and a no-logs policy.

2. **Install the VPN client:** Download and install the VPN client on your computer or other devices you use for work.

3. **Configure the VPN:** Launch the VPN client and follow the setup instructions. You may need to create an account with the VPN provider.

4. **Connect to a server:** Once the VPN client is set up, choose a server location to connect to. Choose a server in your country or a location you trust for the most security and privacy benefits.

5. **Verify the connection:** After connecting to the VPN server, verify that your IP address has changed and that you have a secure connection.

6. **Keep the VPN running:** Keep the VPN client running whenever you use the internet, especially during work-related tasks or when handling sensitive data.

7. **Configure work-related apps:** If you use specific work-related applications or services, ensure they work smoothly with the VPN. Some corporate networks might have restrictions on VPN usage, so check with your IT department if needed.

8. **Update the VPN software:** Regularly update your VPN client to ensure you have the latest security patches and features.

Remember that while VPNs provide significant security benefits, they are not foolproof. Good security practices, such as using strong passwords, keeping your devices updated, and being cautious with email and website links, are essential even when using a VPN. Combining VPN usage with other security measures can create a robust defence against cyber threats while working from your home office.

CHAPTER 5: SECURING YOUR HOME OFFICE INFRASTRUCTURE

Physical Security Measures for Your Workspace

Ensuring physical security in your home office is as important as implementing cybersecurity measures. Physical security helps protect your sensitive information, work-related equipment, and personal belongings from unauthorized access and theft. Here are some physical security measures you can implement in your home office:

1. **Locks and Access Control:** Install sturdy locks on all doors leading to your home office. Consider using deadbolts and smart locks with unique access codes or biometric features for an extra layer of security. Keep spare keys secure and only share access with trusted individuals.

2. **Secure Storage:** Invest in a secure file cabinet or lockable storage unit to store important documents, files, and any physical records containing sensitive information.

3. **Limit Access to Your Workspace:** Dedicate a specific room or area solely to your home office. This helps prevent unauthorized individuals from accessing your work materials and equipment.

4. **Guest Wi-Fi Network:** If visitors are in your home, set up a separate guest Wi-Fi network. This ensures your home office network remains secure and isolated from potential threats.

5. **Screen Privacy Filters:** Consider using a screen privacy filter on your computer monitor to prevent others from viewing your screen from different angles.

6. **Shredder:** Invest in a cross-cut shredder to dispose of sensitive documents properly. Shred any papers that contain personal information, financial details, or sensitive work-related data before discarding them.

7. **Password-Protect Devices:** Use strong passwords or biometric authentication to lock your computer, laptop, and other devices when not in use. Set up automatic screen lock after a period of inactivity.

8. **Physical Cable Security:** Securely route and manage cables to avoid tripping hazards and prevent accidental disconnection of devices. Consider using cable management solutions and desk grommets.

9. **Surveillance Cameras:** Install security cameras in and around your home office to monitor potential security breaches. Ensure you comply with privacy regulations if you're recording video at home.

10. **Home Alarm System:** If possible, connect your home office area to your home's alarm system for added protection against break-ins.

11. **Physical Equipment Locks:** Use security cables and locks to secure laptops physically, monitors, and other valuable equipment to your desk or other fixed objects.

12. **Home Office Insurance:** Consider getting home office insurance or an endorsement to your existing homeowner's insurance policy to cover any potential losses or damages related to your work equipment.

13. **Dispose of Equipment Properly:** When disposing of old equipment or devices, ensure that all data is securely wiped or destroyed to prevent potential data breaches.

14. **Regular Security Audits:** Conduct regular security audits of your home office to identify any weaknesses or areas that require improvement.

By implementing these physical security measures, you can create a safer and more secure workspace in your home office, protecting your work-related assets and your privacy.

Secure Document Management and Disposal

Secure document management and disposal are essential to protect sensitive information in your home office. Mishandling documents can lead to data breaches, identity theft, and other security risks. Here are some guidelines for secure document management and disposal at your home office:

1. **Organize and Label Documents:** Keep your documents organized and categorized based on their sensitivity and importance. Label folders clearly to ensure you can quickly locate and store documents properly.

2. **Use Password Protection and Encryption:** Use strong passwords and encryption to safeguard sensitive information for electronic documents. Consider using file encryption tools or password-protected ZIP files.

3. **Secure Physical Storage:** Invest in a lockable filing cabinet or a secure storage box for physical documents containing sensitive information. Keep the keys or access codes safe and known only to trusted individuals.

4. **Implement a Shredding Policy:** Establish a shredding policy for both paper and electronic documents. Shred physical documents that are no longer needed, especially those containing personal information, financial data, or sensltlve work-related content.

5. **Use a Cross-Cut Shredder:** A cross-cut shredder cuts documents into small confetti-like pieces, making it difficult for anyone to reconstruct the information.

6. **Digitize and Backup:** Consider scanning important documents and storing them securely on encrypted drives or cloud storage. Create backups regularly to avoid data loss.

7. **Limit Access:** Control access to physical and electronic documents. If you have family members or housemates, restrict access to your home office area and lock your computer when you're away.

8. **Dispose of Electronics Securely:** When disposing of old computers, hard drives, or other electronic devices, wipe all data securely or physically destroy the drives before recycling or donating them.

9. **Regularly Review and Purge:** Periodically review your documents and files to determine if they are still necessary. Purge any unnecessary documents to reduce the risk of data exposure.

10. **Be Cautious with Printing:** Avoid printing sensitive documents unless absolutely necessary. If you must print sensitive information, collect the printouts immediately and store them securely.

11. **Keep Software Updated:** Ensure that your document management software, antivirus, and operating system are updated with the latest

security patches to protect against potential vulnerabilities.

12. **Secure Disposal of Physical Documents:** For documents no longer needed, shred them before disposing them in the trash. Alternatively, consider using a secure document disposal service if available in your area.

13. **Secure Digital File Sharing:** When sharing sensitive documents electronically, use secure file-sharing platforms with password protection and encryption features.

14. **Train and Educate:** Educate family members or anyone sharing your home office space about the importance of secure document management and disposal to maintain a secure environment.

By following these practices, you can establish a secure document management and disposal system that protects your sensitive information and reduces the risk of data breaches and identity theft in your home office.

Protecting Printed Documents and Sensitive Information

Protecting printed documents and sensitive information in your home office is crucial to maintaining confidentiality and preventing unauthorized access. Here are some measures you can take to safeguard printed documents and sensitive information:

1. **Secure Storage:** Store printed documents containing sensitive information in a lockable filing cabinet, safe, or secure storage box. Limit access to the key or combination to trusted individuals only.

2. **Minimize Printing:** Whenever possible, avoid printing sensitive information. Opt for digital storage and encryption to reduce the risk of physical document mishandling.

3. **Use Cover Sheets:** When printing sensitive documents, use cover sheets to conceal the content and prevent accidental exposure.

4. **Limit Print Outs:** Print only the number of copies needed. Avoid leaving sensitive documents lying around the office after they are no longer required.

5. **Secure Printing:** If you share your printer with others, set up secure printing features that require a PIN or password to release the print job. This prevents unauthorized access to sensitive documents.

6. **Printer Security:** Keep your printer firmware updated and protect it with a strong administrator password to prevent unauthorized changes or access.

7. **Physically Protect Printers:** Place your printer securely within your home office, away from common areas and external windows.

8. **Secure Disposal:** Shred sensitive documents using a cross-cut shredder before disposing of them. This

includes any draft copies, outdated documents, or papers containing personal information.

9. **Secure Shredder Bin:** Use a designated, lockable shredder bin to collect sensitive documents before shredding. Empty the bin regularly.

10. **Implement a Document Retention Policy:** Establish a document retention policy to determine how long you should keep certain documents. Dispose of documents responsibly after their required retention period expires.

11. **Mark Sensitive Documents:** Clearly label documents containing sensitive information with "Confidential" or "Sensitive" to remind yourself and others of their importance.

12. **Secure Mail Handling:** If you need to send sensitive documents through the mail, use registered or certified mail with tracking to ensure secure delivery.

13. **Secure Document Transport:** When carrying printed sensitive documents outside your home office, use a secure document bag or briefcase.

14. **Educate Family Members:** Educate family members or housemates about respecting your workspace and protecting sensitive documents.

15. **Lock Your Office When Away:** When you leave your home office, lock the room or secure any sensitive documents before you go.

Remember, protecting sensitive information involves a combination of physical and digital security measures. By implementing these practices, you can create a secure environment for handling printed documents and safeguarding sensitive information in your home office.

CHAPTER 6: SECURING COMMUNICATIONS

Encrypted Messaging and Voice Calls

Setting up encrypted messaging and voice calls for a home office is important to ensure the security and privacy of your communication. Here are the steps you can follow to achieve this:

Encrypted Messaging:

1. **Choose a Secure Messaging App:** Several messaging apps offer end-to-end encryption, meaning only you and the recipient can read the messages. Some popular options include Signal, WhatsApp (for personal use), and Telegram (Secret Chats feature).

2. **Install the App:** Download and install the chosen messaging app on your computer and mobile devices.

3. **Create Accounts:** Create accounts on the app using your phone number or email address.

4. **Enable Two-Factor Authentication (2FA):** If the app supports it, enable two-factor authentication for an extra layer of security.

5. **Verify Encryption:** Ensure that the encryption is enabled by default. For example, Signal uses the Signal Protocol for end-to-end encryption.

6. **Add Contacts:** Add your work-related contacts within the app.

7. **Start Messaging:** You can now send encrypted messages to your contacts, ensuring your conversations are secure.

Encrypted Voice Calls:

1. **Choose an Encrypted Voice Call App:** Look for secure voice calls with end-to-end encryption. Signal and WhatsApp are again popular choices for this purpose.

2. **Install the App:** Download and install the app on your devices.

3. **Verify Encryption:** Similar to messaging, verify that voice calls are encrypted end-to-end by default.

4. **Add Contacts:** Ensure your contacts are added within the app.

5. **Initiate Encrypted Voice Calls:** Start voice calls within the app to ensure secure conversations.

Additional Tips:

1. **Device Security:** Ensure your devices (computer, smartphone, tablet) are secure with strong passwords or biometric authentication.

2. **Regular Updates:** Keep the messaging and voice call apps updated to the latest versions to benefit from security patches and improvements.

3. **Network Security:** Ensure your home network is secured with a strong password and WPA3 encryption. This will prevent unauthorized access to your internet connection.

4. **Secure Hardware:** Use devices with trusted hardware and security features if possible.

5. **Avoid Public Networks:** When making sensitive calls or exchanging confidential information, avoid using public Wi-Fi networks, as they might not be secure.

6. **Backup Encryption Keys:** Some encrypted messaging apps allow you to back up your encryption keys. This can be helpful in case you lose your device or need to set up the app on a new device.

7. **Privacy Settings:** Familiarize yourself with the app's privacy settings to control who can contact and see your information.

Remember that while these steps enhance communication security, no system is completely invulnerable. Stay vigilant and cautious when sharing sensitive information.

Securing Video Conferencing and Virtual Meetings

Securing video conferencing and virtual meetings in a home office is crucial to protect your sensitive discussions and ensure privacy. Here's a comprehensive guide to help you achieve this:

1. Choose a Secure Video Conferencing Platform:

Opt for a reputable and secure video conferencing platform. Some popular choices are:

- **Zoom:** Offers end-to-end meeting encryption and provides various security features like meeting passwords and waiting rooms.

- **Microsoft Teams:** Offers encryption, multi-factor authentication, and control over participant permissions.

- **Cisco Webex:** Provides encryption, secure guest access, and host controls.

- **Google Meet:** Offers encryption and security features like meeting codes and guest access controls.

2. Keep the Platform Updated:

Regularly update the video conferencing software to ensure you have the latest security patches and enhancements.

3. Use Strong Meeting IDs and Passwords:

Create strong, unique meeting IDs and passwords for each meeting. Avoid using predictable IDs or passwords to prevent unauthorized access.

4. Enable Waiting Rooms:

Activate the waiting room feature to control who can enter the meeting. This gives you the authority to admit participants individually.

5. Lock Meetings:

Once all expected participants have joined the meeting, lock the meeting to prevent further unauthorized entry.

6. Control Screen Sharing:

Restrict screen sharing to hosts only or specific participants. This prevents unexpected content from being shared.

7. Mute Participants on Entry:

Set the default meeting setting to mute participants upon entry. This prevents background noise or disruptions.

8. Educate Participants:

Educate meeting participants about best practices for virtual meeting security, such as not publicly sharing meeting links and passwords.

9. Encourage Video and Audio Checks:

Ask participants to perform a video and audio check before the meeting starts to address technical issues early on.

10. Avoid Public Links:

Don't share meeting links on public platforms. Instead, send invitations directly to the intended participants.

11. Use VPN for Added Security:

Consider using a Virtual Private Network (VPN) to encrypt your internet connection and add an extra layer of security.

12. Secure Your Device:

Ensure your computer and devices are protected with strong passwords, biometric authentication, and up-to-date security software.

13. Be Wary of Recordings:

If you record meetings, store recordings in secure locations and only share them with authorized individuals.

14. Test Security Settings:

Conduct test meetings to ensure security settings are configured correctly before important meetings.

15. Privacy and Data Handling:

Review the platform's privacy policy and data handling practices to understand how your information is used and stored.

16. Regularly Review Security Updates:

Stay informed about security updates and new features the video conferencing platform provides and implement them as needed.

By following these steps and maintaining awareness of security best practices, you can significantly enhance the security and privacy of virtual meetings and video conferences in your home office.

Avoiding Social Engineering Attacks

Avoiding social engineering attacks in a home office environment is essential to protect sensitive information and maintain cybersecurity. Here are steps you can take to prevent falling victim to these types of attacks:

1. Educate Yourself and Your Team:

- Learn about different types of social engineering attacks, such as phishing, pretexting, baiting, and tailgating.

- Educate your family members or anyone sharing your home office space about the importance of cybersecurity and how to recognize suspicious activities.

2. Be Skeptical of Unsolicited Communication:

- Be cautious when receiving emails, phone calls, or messages from unknown or unexpected sources.

- Verify the sender's identity before responding to requests for sensitive information or actions.

3. Verify Requests for Information:

- Always verify the legitimacy of requests for sensitive information, even if they appear to come from trusted sources.

- Use official contact information from established sources rather than clicking on links or using contact details from unsolicited messages.

4. Strengthen Email Security:

- Use strong, unique passwords for your email accounts.

- Enable multi-factor authentication (MFA) for an additional layer of security.

- Be cautious of email attachments and links, especially if they ask for login credentials or personal information.

5. Use Strong Passwords and MFA:

- Implement strong, unique passwords for all your accounts.

- Enable multi-factor authentication wherever possible to prevent unauthorized access.

6. Secure Your Wi-Fi Network:

- Use a strong, unique password for your Wi-Fi network.

- Enable WPA3 encryption if supported for stronger security.

7. Regularly Update Software:

- Keep your operating system, applications, and security software up to date to ensure you have the latest security patches.

8. Install Reliable Security Software:

- Install reputable antivirus and anti-malware software to detect and prevent potential threats.

9. Beware of Impersonation:

- Be cautious of anyone claiming to be a colleague, supervisor, or IT support asking for sensitive information.

- Verify such requests through official channels before complying.

10. Limit Information Sharing on Social Media:

- Avoid sharing personal or sensitive information on social media platforms that attackers can use to craft convincing social engineering attacks.

11. Be Cautious of Pop-ups and Advertisements:

- Avoid clicking on pop-ups or advertisements that ask for personal information or appear suspicious.

12. Train and Test Your Team:

- Conduct regular cybersecurity training for yourself and anyone who shares your home office space.

- Test your team's ability to recognize and respond to social engineering attacks through simulated phishing exercises.

13. Stay Informed:

- Keep up to date with the latest cybersecurity news and trends to be aware of new tactics used in social engineering attacks.

14. Report Suspicious Activity:

- If you encounter a suspicious email, message, or phone call, report it to your IT department, service provider, or relevant authorities.

Following these practices and maintaining a cautious and vigilant mindset can significantly reduce the risk of falling victim to social engineering attacks in your home office.

CHAPTER 7: SOFTWARE AND APPLICATION SECURITY

Managing Software and App Permissions

Managing software and app permissions in a home office is crucial to maintaining security and privacy. Here's a guide on how to effectively manage permissions for the software and apps you use:

1. Regularly Review Installed Software and Apps:

Regularly review the software and apps installed on your devices. Uninstall any you no longer use or need, as unnecessary software can increase your attack surface.

2. Keep Software and Apps Updated:

Regularly update your software and apps to ensure you have the latest security patches and bug fixes. Outdated software can be vulnerable to attacks.

3. Limit Administrative Privileges:

Use a standard user account for day-to-day tasks rather than an administrator account. This limits the potential damage if malware or malicious software is inadvertently installed.

4. Use Trusted Sources for Software:

Only download and install software from reputable sources. Avoid downloading software from unofficial websites or unverified sources.

5. Review and Adjust App Permissions:

For apps on your mobile devices and computers:

- Review the permissions requested by each app during installation or use.

- Grant only the necessary permissions. If an app requests access to more data or functions than it needs, deny those permissions.

6. Mobile Device App Permissions:

- On mobile devices, review and adjust app permissions in your device settings.

- For example, you can control which apps can access your location, camera, microphone, contacts, etc.

7. Computer App Permissions:

- On computers, modern operating systems prompt you to allow or deny certain permissions when an app is launched for the first time.

- You can also review and modify these permissions in your system settings.

8. Review Privacy Policies:

- Before installing an app, review its privacy policy to understand how your data will be collected, used, and shared.

- Avoid apps that require excessive data sharing or use vague privacy terms.

9. Use App Store and Official Repositories:

- Download apps from official app stores (like Apple App Store and Google Play Store) or official repositories (like Microsoft Store Ubuntu Software) to reduce the risk of malicious software.

10. Disable Unneeded Features:

- Some apps come with features you might not use. Disable or turn off features that aren't necessary to reduce potential attack vectors.

11. Regularly Review and Update Permissions:

- Periodically review and update app permissions as your needs change.

- Remove permissions from apps you no longer use.

12. Be Cautious of Third-Party Integrations:

- When using software or apps that integrate with third-party services, review the permissions you're granting to those services.

13. Use Security Software:

- Install and regularly update antivirus and anti-malware software to scan for potentially harmful software.

14. Educate Yourself and Your Family:

- Educate everyone using your home office about the importance of reviewing and managing app permissions.

15. Be Mindful of Browser Extensions:

- Be cautious when installing browser extensions. Only use trusted extensions from reputable sources.

By carefully managing software and app permissions, you can reduce the risk of unauthorized access, data breaches, and other security vulnerabilities in your home office environment.

Keeping Software Updated and Secure

Managing software and app permissions in a home office is crucial to maintaining security and privacy. Here's a guide on how to effectively manage permissions for the software and apps you use:

1. Regularly Review Installed Software and Apps:

Regularly review the software and apps installed on your devices. Uninstall any you no longer use or need, as unnecessary software can increase your attack surface.

2. Keep Software and Apps Updated:

Regularly update your software and apps to ensure you have the latest security patches and bug fixes. Outdated software can be vulnerable to attacks.

3. Limit Administrative Privileges:

Use a standard user account for day-to-day tasks rather than an administrator account. This limits the potential damage if malware or malicious software is inadvertently installed.

4. Use Trusted Sources for Software:

Only download and install software from reputable sources. Avoid downloading software from unofficial websites or unverified sources.

5. Review and Adjust App Permissions:

For apps on your mobile devices and computers:

- Review the permissions requested by each app during installation or use.

- Grant only the necessary permissions. If an app requests access to more data or functions than it needs, deny those permissions.

6. Mobile Device App Permissions:

- On mobile devices, review and adjust app permissions in your device settings.

- For example, you can control which apps can access your location, camera, microphone, contacts, etc.

7. Computer App Permissions:

- On computers, modern operating systems prompt you to allow or deny certain permissions when an app is launched for the first time.

- You can also review and modify these permissions in your system settings.

8. Review Privacy Policies:

- Before installing an app, review its privacy policy to understand how your data will be collected, used, and shared.

- Avoid apps that require excessive data sharing or use vague privacy terms.

9. Use App Store and Official Repositories:

- Download apps from official app stores (like Apple App Store and Google Play Store) or official repositories (like Microsoft Store Ubuntu Software) to reduce the risk of malicious software.

10. Disable Unneeded Features:

- Some apps come with features you might not use. Disable or turn off features that aren't necessary to reduce potential attack vectors.

11. Regularly Review and Update Permissions:

- Periodically review and update app permissions as your needs change.

- Remove permissions from apps you no longer use.

12. Be Cautious of Third-Party Integrations:

- When using software or apps that integrate with third-party services, review the permissions you're granting to those services.

13. Use Security Software:

- Install and regularly update antivirus and anti-malware software to scan for potentially harmful software.

14. Educate Yourself and Your Family:

- Educate everyone using your home office about the importance of reviewing and managing app permissions.

15. Be Mindful of Browser Extensions:

- Be cautious when installing browser extensions. Only use trusted extensions from reputable sources.

By carefully managing software and app permissions, you can reduce the risk of unauthorized access, data breaches, and other security vulnerabilities in your home office environment.

Keeping Software Updated and Secure at home office

Keeping software updated and secure in your home office is essential for maintaining the security of your digital environment. Here's a comprehensive guide to help you achieve this:

1. Enable Automatic Updates:

- Enable automatic updates for your operating system, software applications, and antivirus/anti-malware programs. This ensures you receive the latest security patches without manual intervention.

2. Keep Your Operating System Updated:

- Regularly update your operating system (Windows, macOS, Linux) to receive security patches, bug fixes, and performance improvements.

3. Update Software Applications:

- Update all installed software applications, including web browsers, productivity software, media players, and any other tools you use.

- Many software applications have built-in update mechanisms. Enable these options or set the software to notify you when updates are available.

4. Keep Hardware Drivers Up to Date:

- Update hardware drivers for components like graphics cards, network adapters, and printers. Outdated drivers can lead to security vulnerabilities and compatibility issues.

5. Remove Unnecessary Software:

- Regularly review your installed software and uninstall applications you no longer use. Unused software can become a security risk if not updated.

6. Use Legitimate Sources:

- Download software from official websites or authorized app stores to avoid malicious or compromised versions.

7. Secure Your Web Browsing:

- Keep your web browser up to date. Browsers often contain security fixes that protect against vulnerabilities.

- Use browser extensions or add-ons that block malicious websites and scripts.

8. Regularly Check for Updates:

- Even if automatic updates are enabled, periodically check for updates manually to ensure nothing is missed.

9. Prioritize Critical Updates:

- Pay special attention to critical security updates that address known vulnerabilities. These should be installed as soon as possible.

10. Backup Your Data:

- Regularly back up your important data to an external drive or cloud storage. You'll have a copy of your data in case of a security breach or system failure.

11. Implement Multi-Factor Authentication (MFA):

- Whenever possible, enable multi-factor authentication for your online accounts. This adds an extra layer of security even if your password is compromised.

12. Use Antivirus and Anti-Malware Software:

- Install reputable antivirus and anti-malware software to protect against viruses, malware, and other threats.

13. Secure Your Network:

- Use a strong and unique Wi-Fi password to prevent unauthorized access to your network.
- Implement network security protocols like WPA3 for stronger encryption.

14. Educate Yourself:

- Stay informed about the latest cybersecurity threats and best practices. Understand common attack vectors like phishing and ransomware.

15. Set Up a Schedule:

- Create a regular schedule to review and apply updates. This could be weekly or monthly, depending on your preferences and needs.

16. Test Updates in a Safe Environment:

- For major updates or software changes, consider testing them in a controlled environment before applying them to your main setup.

By following these steps, you can significantly reduce the risk of security breaches and ensure the software and applications in your home office remain up-to-date and secure.

Using Antivirus and Anti-malware Solutions

Using antivirus and anti-malware solutions in your home office is crucial to protecting your devices and data from various cyber threats. Here's how to effectively utilize these security tools:

1. Choose Reputable Software:

Select a well-known and reputable antivirus and anti-malware software from established vendors. Some popular options include Norton, McAfee, Bitdefender, Kaspersky, and Windows Defender (built into Windows).

2. Install and Update:

- Install the antivirus and anti-malware software on all your devices, including computers, laptops, and mobile devices.

- Enable automatic updates to ensure you have the latest virus definitions and security patches.

3. Real-Time Scanning:

Activate real-time scanning, which constantly monitors files, downloads, and activities on your devices to identify and block threats as they occur.

4. Regular Scans:

Schedule regular full system scans to thoroughly check your device for any existing malware or viruses that might have evaded real-time protection.

5. USB and External Device Scanning:

Enable the option to scan USB drives, external hard drives, and other external devices for malware before opening or accessing their contents.

6. Browser Extensions:

Use browser extensions provided by some antivirus solutions to help detect and block malicious websites and phishing attempts.

7. Email Protection:

Choose an antivirus solution that offers email protection to help identify and block malicious attachments and links in your email messages.

8. Behavior-Based Detection:

Look for antivirus software that includes behavior-based detection. This technology can identify suspicious behaviour and activity that traditional signature-based scans may not catch.

9. Safe Browsing:

Avoid clicking on suspicious links or downloading files from untrustworthy sources. Even with antivirus protection, safe browsing habits are essential.

10. Regular Updates:

Keep the antivirus and anti-malware software itself up to date by regularly checking for updates or enabling automatic updates.

11. Configure Settings:

- Review the software's settings to ensure it's configured according to your security preferences.
- Adjust settings for scans, notifications, and other security features the software offers.

12. Avoid Running Multiple Solutions:

Running multiple antivirus or anti-malware solutions simultaneously can lead to conflicts and performance issues. Stick to one reliable solution.

13. Educate Yourself:

Understand the types of threats the software protects against and how it works. This knowledge can help you recognize potential risks and make informed decisions.

14. Regularly Review Reports:

Regularly review the reports generated by the antivirus software. These reports provide insights into detected threats and overall system health.

15. Keep Operating Systems Updated:

Combine antivirus and anti-malware protection while keeping your operating system and software applications current to ensure comprehensive security.

Remember that while antivirus and anti-malware solutions are essential components of cybersecurity, they are not foolproof. Safe online behaviour and a layered security approach are equally important to protect your home office environment from threats.

CHAPTER 8: ESTABLISHING A SECURITY POLICY FOR FAMILY MEMBERS AND GUESTS

Secure Access for Guests in Your Home Office

Providing secure access for guests in your home office involves setting up a controlled environment that allows temporary access without compromising the security of your personal and work-related information. Here's how to do it:

1. Guest Network:

- Set up a separate guest Wi-Fi network with a strong password. This network should be isolated from your main network, preventing guests from accessing your devices and sensitive information.

2. Enable Guest Mode on Devices:

- For devices that support it, enable guest mode. This limits the access guests have to your personal accounts and data.

3. Use a Guest Account:

- Create a guest account on your computer if supported by your operating system. This account should have limited privileges and access to only certain files and applications.

4. Limit Device Access:

- If possible, provide guests with a dedicated computer or device with limited access to your personal files and information.

5. Temporary User Profiles:

- If you can't create a guest account, consider creating a temporary user profile with limited guest access on your computer.

6. Screen Locking:

- Set your computer to lock after a certain period of inactivity. This prevents unauthorized access if you step away from your workspace.

7. Use Passwords and PINs:

- Password-protect devices, files, and accounts. Encourage guests to use strong PINs or passwords to access certain resources.

8. Provide Specific Permissions:

- If guests need to use certain applications or files, provide them with specific permissions instead of full access to your system.

9. Supervision:

- Whenever possible, supervise guests while using your workspace to ensure they don't access anything they shouldn't.

10. Educate Guests:

- Inform your guests about the importance of respecting your privacy and the security measures you have in place.

11. Limited Time Access:

- Set a limit on how long guests can access your workspace, and ensure they log out or disconnect after their session.

12. Clear Browser Cache and Cookies:

- If guests use your computer to browse the internet, clear the browser cache and cookies after their session to prevent them from accessing your accounts.

13. Guest Agreements:

- If you frequently have guests using your home office, consider creating a simple agreement outlining the rules and expectations for using your workspace.

14. Secure Your Physical Space:

- Ensure that your physical workspace is locked when not in use to prevent unauthorized access.

15. Review Permissions Afterward:

- After a guest has used your workspace, review and reset any permissions or access they were granted.

By implementing these measures, you can offer secure access to guests in your home office without compromising the security of your personal and work-related information.

CHAPTER 9: MONITORING AND RESPONDING TO SECURITY INCIDENTS

Detecting Suspicious Activities and Intrusions

Detecting suspicious activities and intrusions in your home office is crucial for maintaining cybersecurity. Here's how to effectively monitor and identify potential threats:

1. Network Monitoring:

- Use network monitoring tools to track traffic and identify unusual patterns or unexpected connections.

2. Intrusion Detection System (IDS):

- Set up an IDS to monitor network traffic for signs of unauthorized access, abnormal behaviour, or known attack patterns.

3. Firewall Alerts:

- Configure your firewall to send alerts for unusual or suspicious activity, such as repeated connection attempts.

4. Security Software Alerts:

- Enable notifications from your antivirus and anti-malware software to receive alerts about detected threats.

5. Account Activity:

- Regularly review the activity logs of your accounts (email, social media, etc.) for any unfamiliar logins or unauthorized actions.

6. Unusual Device Behavior:

- Monitor the behaviour of your devices. Sudden slowdowns, crashes, or strange activities might indicate a compromise.

7. Email Safety:

- Be cautious of phishing emails and suspicious attachments. Report them to your email provider.

8. Use Security Tools:

- Utilize intrusion detection tools, network analyzers, and traffic monitoring tools to identify potential threats.

9. Anomaly Detection:

- Implement anomaly detection mechanisms to identify deviations from regular behaviour in your digital environment.

10. Strong Password Policies:

- Use strong, unique passwords and enable multi-factor authentication for accounts to prevent unauthorized access.

11. Regular Software Updates:

- Keep your operating system and software applications updated to protect against known vulnerabilities.

12. Monitor Cloud Services:

- If you use cloud services, monitor account activity and configure alerts for unusual actions.

13. Use Virtual Private Networks (VPNs):

- When accessing sensitive information remotely, use a VPN to encrypt your connection and protect against eavesdropping.

14. Set Up Alerts:

- Configure alerts for any unauthorized login attempts or changes in system settings.

15. Employee Training:

- Educate anyone who uses your home office about cybersecurity best practices to prevent accidental security breaches.

16. Behavior Analysis:

- Keep an eye on user behaviour patterns. Sudden changes in activity could indicate an issue.

17. Review Logs:

- Regularly review logs from security systems, firewalls, and antivirus software for any signs of unusual activity.

18. Stay Informed:

- Stay updated on the latest cybersecurity threats and techniques to recognize potential risks better.

19. Security Audit:

- Periodically conduct a security audit of your home office environment to identify vulnerabilities and weaknesses.

20. Consider Professional Help:

- If you're concerned about security, consider hiring a professional to assess and enhance your home office security.

By implementing these measures and staying vigilant, you can detect and address suspicious activities and potential intrusions in your home office before they escalate into security breaches.

Creating an Incident Response Plan

Creating an incident response plan for your home office is essential to be prepared for cybersecurity incidents and effectively mitigate their impact. Here's a step-by-step guide to help you develop a comprehensive incident response plan:

1. Identify Key Assets:

- List the critical assets, devices, data, and applications in your home office that need protection.

2. Define Incident Types:

- Identify potential cybersecurity incidents affecting your home office, such as data breaches, malware infections, phishing attacks, or unauthorized access.

3. Establish a Response Team:

- Designate individuals who will be part of your incident response team. This could include yourself, family members, or any IT professionals you may collaborate with.

4. Communication Plan:

- Define how your response team will communicate during an incident. Establish communication channels, methods, and points of contact.

5. Incident Detection:

- Detail how you will detect incidents. This could involve using security tools, monitoring logs, and setting up alerts.

6. Incident Assessment:

- Describe how you will assess the severity and impact of an incident on your home office operations.

7. Incident Containment:

- Outline the steps you will take to contain the incident and prevent further spread or damage.

8. Eradication and Recovery:

- Specify the actions you will take to remove the threat, malware, or unauthorized access from your systems, followed by the steps to recover your systems to normal operation.

9. Data Breach Notification:

- If you handle personal or sensitive data, detail how you will handle data breach incidents, including notifying affected parties as necessary.

10. Documentation:

- Create templates for incident reporting, documenting actions taken and any evidence collected during the incident.

11. Legal and Regulatory Compliance:

- Understand and outline any legal or regulatory requirements related to incident reporting, data breaches, or data protection.

12. Regular Testing and Training:

- Schedule regular drills to simulate incidents and practice your response plan. Train your response team on the plan's procedures.

13. Recovery Plan:

- Detail how you will recover your systems and data after an incident, including data restoration, system testing, and validation.

14. Continuous Improvement:

- Establish a process to regularly review and update the incident response plan to adapt to evolving threats and changes in your home office environment.

15. Resources and Contacts:

- Compile a list of contacts for external support, such as IT professionals, cybersecurity experts, or law enforcement, in case you need assistance during a severe incident.

16. Post-Incident Analysis:

- After each incident, conduct a post-incident analysis to identify areas for improvement and implement necessary changes.

17. Public Communication Plan:

- If your incident has the potential to impact clients, partners, or customers, develop a communication strategy for addressing their concerns.

18. Offline Backup:

- Keep an offline backup of critical files and data that can be used to recover from incidents like ransomware attacks.

Remember that your home office incident response plan should be tailored to your needs and environment. It's important to ensure that everyone in your home office environment is aware of the plan and their roles in case of an incident.

Reporting Cybersecurity Incidents

Reporting cybersecurity incidents for your home office is essential to mitigate the impact of potential threats and breaches. Here's how you can effectively report cybersecurity incidents:

1. Document the Incident:

- Immediately start documenting all relevant details of the incident. This includes the date and time of the incident, what happened, how it happened, and any suspicious activities or behaviours you observed.

2. Assess the Severity:

- Determine the severity of the incident. Is it a minor issue or a significant breach that requires immediate attention?

3. Isolate Affected Systems:

- If possible, isolate the affected systems or devices from your network to prevent the incident from spreading further.

4. Contact IT or Security Professionals:

- If you have IT professionals or cybersecurity experts, you can consult and contact them for guidance and assistance.

5. Notify Relevant Parties:

- If the incident involves personal data or affects others, you may need to notify affected parties about the breach. Check the relevant laws and regulations for your jurisdiction.

6. Contact Your Internet Service Provider (ISP):

- If the incident involves significant network issues, contact your ISP for assistance and to check if they have any insights about the incident.

7. Use Trusted Channels:

- Use trusted communication channels to report the incident. Avoid using the same compromised channels that were used during the incident.

8. Report to Relevant Authorities:

- If the incident is severe and involves illegal activities, consider reporting it to appropriate law enforcement agencies.

9. Online Reporting Portals:

- Many countries have online reporting portals for cybersecurity incidents. Check if your country has one and report the incident if necessary.

10. Contact Software and Service Providers:

- If the incident involves software or services you use, contact the respective providers to report the issue and seek assistance.

11. Preserve Evidence:

- Keep records, logs, screenshots, or any evidence related to the incident. This can help with investigations and reporting.

12. Maintain Communication:

- Keep communication lines open with IT professionals, security experts, and any authorities to whom you've reported the incident.

13. Implement Mitigation Measures:

- Based on the recommendations of professionals, implement mitigation measures to prevent further damage and secure your systems.

14. Inform Affected Parties:

- If personal data or sensitive information has been compromised, inform affected parties about the breach, the steps you're taking to address it, and any recommended actions they should take.

15. Learn from the Incident:

- After resolving the incident, conduct a post-incident analysis to understand how it happened, what measures were effective, and how to improve your cybersecurity measures.

Timely reporting of cybersecurity incidents is crucial to prevent further damage and protect your home office environment. It's important to act swiftly and follow appropriate procedures to handle the incident effectively.

CHAPTER 10: CYBERSECURITY BEST PRACTICES FOR REMOTE WORK

Balancing Productivity and Security

Enhancing productivity and security in your home office environment is essential to create a workspace that is efficient, functional, and well-protected. Here are some tips to help you achieve this balance:

1. Set Up a Dedicated Workspace:

- Designate a specific area in your home for work. This helps create a clear boundary between work and personal life while enhancing security by keeping work-related activities contained.

2. Use Secure Connections:

- Ensure that your Wi-Fi network is secure with a strong password and uses encryption (preferably WPA3). This prevents unauthorized access to your network.

3. Keep Software Updated:

- Regularly update your operating system, software applications, and security tools to protect against vulnerabilities and exploits.

4. Use Trusted Tools and Services:

- Choose reputable software, tools, and cloud services that have strong security measures in place.

5. Implement Multi-Factor Authentication (MFA):

- Enable MFA for your important accounts and applications to add an extra layer of security without compromising productivity.

6. Backup Your Data:

- Regularly back up your work-related data to an external drive or secure cloud storage. This protects your data from loss due to hardware failures, accidents, or security incidents.

7. Use a VPN for Remote Access:

- If you need to access your work network remotely, use a Virtual Private Network (VPN) to encrypt your connection and ensure secure access.

8. Password Management:

- Use a password manager to generate strong, unique passwords for your accounts while maintaining easy access to them.

9. Secure Video Conferencing:

- Implement security practices for virtual meetings, such as using passwords, enabling waiting rooms, and sharing meeting links securely.

10. Educate Yourself and Family Members:

- Educate your family members about the importance of maintaining security measures and respecting your work-related boundaries.

11. Secure Physical Workspace:

- Lock your workspace when not in use to prevent unauthorized access. Use privacy screens on devices to prevent others from viewing sensitive information.

12. Regularly Review Permissions:

- Review the permissions granted to apps, software, and services to ensure they have the minimum necessary access.

13. Avoid Public Wi-Fi for Work:

- When working outside your home office, avoid using public Wi-Fi networks for work-related tasks due to potential security risks.

14. Avoid Email Phishing:

- Be cautious of emails requesting sensitive information or instructing you to take actions like clicking on links or downloading attachments. Verify the sender's identity before taking any action.

15. Time Management:

- Create a schedule that includes dedicated work hours and regular breaks to maintain productivity while preventing burnout.

16. Regular Security Audits:

- Periodically conduct security audits of your home office environment to identify vulnerabilities and weaknesses.

Balancing productivity and security requires a proactive approach. By implementing these strategies, you can create a home office environment that promotes efficiency while safeguarding sensitive information and maintaining a secure workspace.

Using Secure File Sharing and Collaboration Tools

Using secure file sharing and collaboration tools is crucial for maintaining the confidentiality and integrity of your work in a home office environment. Here are steps you can take to ensure secure file sharing and collaboration:

1. Choose Trusted Tools:

- Select reputable file-sharing and collaboration platforms prioritizing security and offering end-to-end encryption.

2. Enable Two-Factor Authentication (2FA):

- Enable 2FA for your accounts on these platforms to add an extra layer of security.

3. Use Strong Passwords:

- Use strong, unique passwords for your accounts and regularly update them.

4. End-to-End Encryption:

- Use platforms that offer end-to-end encryption, ensuring only authorized parties can access the shared content.

5. Control Access Levels:

- Use platforms that allow you to set granular access controls. Only grant necessary permissions to collaborators.

6. Secure Sharing Links:

- If sharing links, ensure they are password-protected or have expiration dates. Avoid public sharing if possible.

7. Version Control:

- Use tools that support version control to keep track of changes and revisions made to shared files.

8. Avoid Public Wi-Fi:

- Avoid using public Wi-Fi networks to access or share sensitive files, as they can be vulnerable to attacks.

9. Regularly Update Software:

- Keep the file-sharing and collaboration tools updated to benefit from the latest security patches and enhancements.

10. Educate Collaborators:

- Educate anyone you collaborate with about security practices, including using strong passwords, not sharing credentials, and recognizing phishing attempts.

11. Secure File Uploads:

- Scan files for malware before uploading them to the platform to prevent spreading infections.

12. Monitor Account Activity:

- Regularly review account activity and set up alerts for any suspicious actions.

13. Disable Unused Features:

- If the platform has features you don't use, consider disabling them to reduce potential security risks.

14. Protect Devices:

- Ensure that the devices you use for collaboration are secured with strong passwords, biometric authentication, and up-to-date security software.

15. Backup Data:

- Regularly back up your shared files to an external drive or secure cloud storage to prevent data loss.

16. Secure Video Conferencing:

- If your collaboration involves video conferencing, ensure the platform you use employs security measures like encryption and password protection.

17. Review Terms and Conditions:

- Understand the terms of service and privacy policies of the platforms you use to ensure they align with your security and privacy needs.

18. Test Security Features:

- Familiarize yourself with the security features of your chosen platform through testing and experimentation.

By following these steps and using secure file-sharing and collaboration tools, you can work efficiently with colleagues and collaborators while maintaining the highest level of security for your work-related information.

Securing Personal Devices Used for Work

Securing personal devices used for work in a home office is crucial to protecting sensitive information and maintaining cybersecurity. Here's how to secure personal devices effectively:

1. Use Strong Passwords or Biometric Authentication:

- Set up strong and unique passwords for your devices. Consider using biometric authentication like fingerprint or facial recognition if available.

2. Enable Full Disk Encryption:

- Encrypt the entire device's storage to prevent unauthorized access to your data in case the device is lost or stolen.

3. Regularly Update Software:

- Keep your operating system, applications, and security software updated with the latest security patches.

4. Use Reputable Security Software:

- Install reputable antivirus and anti-malware software to protect against viruses, malware, and other threats.

5. Separate Work and Personal Data:

- Create separate user accounts for work and personal use. This helps maintain privacy and prevent work-related data from mingling with personal information.

6. Implement Strong Network Security:

- Use a strong and unique Wi-Fi password for your home network. Consider using WPA3 encryption for better security.

7. Use a Virtual Private Network (VPN):

- If accessing work-related resources remotely, use a VPN to encrypt your internet connection and ensure data privacy.

8. Secure Remote Desktop Access:

- If using remote desktop or screen-sharing tools, ensure they are secure and require strong authentication.

9. Lock Devices When Idle:

- Set up your devices to lock automatically after a period of inactivity to prevent unauthorized access.

10. Disable Unnecessary Features:

- Disable features, services, or apps you don't use to reduce potential attack vectors.

11. Secure Browser Settings:

- Configure your web browser with privacy and security settings, and use browser extensions to block malicious content.

12. Regularly Backup Data:

- Regularly back up your data to an external drive or secure cloud storage. This ensures data recovery in case of device failure or loss.

13. Be Wary of Downloads:

- Only download software, apps, and files from reputable sources. Avoid downloading from unfamiliar websites or emails.

14. Educate Family Members:

- Educate your family members about the importance of cybersecurity and the need to respect the security measures in place on your devices.

15. Secure Video Conferencing:

- If using personal devices for video conferencing, ensure the applications are updated and secure to prevent unauthorized access.

16. Review and Control App Permissions:

- Regularly review and restrict app permissions to prevent unnecessary access to your personal data.

17. Enable Remote Wipe and Find My Device:

- Activate features that allow you to remotely wipe your device's data if lost or stolen and use "Find My Device" features to track its location.

By following these steps, you can significantly enhance the security of your personal devices used for work in your home office, minimizing the risk of unauthorized access and data breaches.

CHAPTER 11: CHILDREN AND CYBERSECURITY

Childproofing Devices and Internet Access

Childproofing devices and controlling internet access in your home office are crucial to ensure a safe and productive environment for both work and family. Here are steps you can take to childproof devices and manage internet access:

1. Create Separate User Accounts:

- Set up separate user accounts on your devices for you and your children. This helps keep your work-related data separate from their activities.

2. Use Parental Control Software:

- Install parental control software or tools that allow you to set content filters screen time limits, and monitor your children's online activities.

3. Enable Parental Controls on Devices:

- Many devices, including computers, smartphones, and tablets, have built-in parental control settings. Activate these features to restrict access and content.

4. Password-Protect Devices:

- Lock your devices with strong passwords, PINs, or biometric authentication to prevent unauthorized access by children.

5. Secure Browsers:

- Use web browsers with parental control extensions or settings that block inappropriate content and filter search results.

6. Set Up Child-Friendly Accounts:

- If your children need access to devices, create child-friendly user accounts with limited privileges and access to only approved apps.

7. Use Safe Search Settings:

- Enable safe search settings on search engines to filter out explicit content from search results.

8. Configure Router Settings:

- Access your router's settings and set up content filtering, time limits, and internet usage controls for specific devices.

9. Network-Level Protection:

- Consider using a DNS filtering service or a family-friendly router with built-in parental controls to manage internet access.

10. Monitor Online Activities:

- Regularly review your children's online activities to ensure they are using devices and the internet safely.

11. Educate Your Children:

- Teach your children about online safety, the importance of not sharing personal information, and recognizing potentially harmful content.

12. Set Screen Time Limits:

- Establish rules for screen time and ensure your children have a healthy balance between online and offline activities.

13. Create a Safe Workspace:

- Organize your home office to keep cords, plugs, and devices out of your children's reach to avoid accidents.

14. Lock Away Devices:

- When not using your devices, keep them stored securely to prevent your children from accessing them without supervision.

15. Regularly Review and Update Settings:

- As your children grow and their needs change, update your parental control settings and guidelines accordingly.

16. Discuss Online Etiquette:

- Teach your children about appropriate online behaviour, including communicating respectfully and responsibly.

17. Be a Role Model:

- Demonstrate responsible device and internet usage yourself, as children often learn by observing adults.

By implementing these measures, you can create a home office environment that is child-friendly and conducive to both work and family life while ensuring your children's safety and well-being online.

Monitoring and Managing Children's Online Activities

Monitoring and managing your children's online activities in your home office is important to ensure their safety and responsible internet use. Here's how you can effectively monitor and manage their online activities:

1. Open Communication:

- Talk to your children about internet safety, responsible online behaviour, and the potential risks they may encounter.

2. Set Clear Rules:

- Establish rules and guidelines for using devices and the internet, including screen time limits, appropriate websites, and online interactions.

3. Use Parental Control Software:

- Install parental control software on devices your children use. These tools allow you to filter content, set screen time limits, and monitor their activities.

4. Enable Safe Search and Filters:

- Enable safe search settings on search engines to filter out explicit content. Use content filters on browsers and apps to block inappropriate websites.

5. Create Child-Friendly Profiles:

- If your devices allow it, create separate user profiles for your children with limited access to apps and settings.

6. Monitor Social Media Usage:

- If your children use social media, discuss the platforms they're on and set privacy settings to restrict who can view their posts.

7. Monitor App Downloads:

- Monitor the apps your children download and use. Make sure they understand the importance of only downloading from trusted sources.

8. Educate About Sharing Personal Information:

- Teach your children not to share personal information online, including their full name, address, school, and contact details.

9. Monitor Online Friends:

- If your children engage in online gaming or social networks, ensure they only connect with people they know.

10. Regularly Review Browsing History:

- Periodically review device browsing history to understand what your children are accessing online.

11. Use Screen Time Management:

- Utilize built-in device features or third-party apps to manage and limit screen time for different activities.

12. Encourage Offline Activities:

- Encourage your children to engage in offline activities like reading, playing outdoors, and spending time with family.

13. Lead by Example:

- Demonstrate responsible online behaviour to set a positive example for your children.

14. Have Tech-Free Zones:

- Designate specific areas or times where devices are not allowed in your home, promoting face-to-face interactions.

15. Review and Adjust as Needed:

- Continuously assess and adjust your monitoring and rules based on your children's age, maturity, and changing online habits.

16. Address Online Bullying:

- Teach your children about the importance of reporting and discussing any instances of online bullying or harassment they encounter.

17. Foster Trust:

- Create an environment where your children feel comfortable discussing any concerns or questions they have about their online experiences.

Balancing technology use with responsible online behaviour and offline activities is essential to ensure your children's safety and well-being. At the same time, they interact with the digital world in your home office environment.

Educating Children about Online Safety

Educating children about online safety is crucial to help them navigate the digital world responsibly and protect themselves from potential risks. Here's how you can effectively educate your children about online safety in your home office:

1. Start Early:

- Begin educating your children about online safety when using devices and the internet.

2. Use Age-Appropriate Language:

- Tailor your discussions to your children's age and understanding. Use simple language and examples they can relate to.

3. Teach Personal Information Protection:

- Explain to your children why they shouldn't share personal information like their full name, address, school, phone number, or passwords online.

4. Online Privacy:

- Teach them about the importance of privacy settings on social media platforms, online games, and other websites.

5. Recognizing Strangers:

- Help them understand that not everyone online is who they claim to be. Teach them not to communicate with or share information with strangers.

6. Cyberbullying Awareness:

- Discuss what cyberbullying is and encourage them to talk to you if they encounter any form of online harassment.

7. Identifying Phishing and Scams:

- Teach them to recognize suspicious emails, messages, and pop-ups and to avoid clicking on links or sharing personal information.

8. Safe Online Interaction:

- Discuss appropriate online behaviour, including respecting others, being kind, and avoiding hurtful comments or actions.

9. Importance of Reporting:

- Encourage them to report inappropriate or uncomfortable interactions to you or a trusted adult.

10. Avoiding Malicious Downloads:

- Teach them not to download files, apps, or software from untrusted sources, as they might contain viruses or malware.

11. Managing Social Media:

- Discuss the potential consequences of sharing personal information and photos on social media and help them set privacy settings.

12. Critical Thinking Online:

- Teach them to question the accuracy of information they come across online and to verify facts from reliable sources.

13. Online Etiquette:

- Discuss the importance of being polite and respectful in online conversations, just as they would be in person.

14. Set Screen Time Limits:

- Establish clear rules for screen time and device usage and explain the reasons behind them.

15. Learning to Disconnect:

- Help them understand the importance of balancing online and offline activities, like spending time with family and friends.

16. Encourage Open Communication:

- Create an environment where your children feel comfortable discussing their online experiences and asking questions.

17. Regular Check-Ins:

- Periodically discuss their online activities and ask if they've encountered anything that made them uncomfortable.

18. Be a Role Model:

- Demonstrate responsible online behaviour yourself, as children learn from observing adults.

Educating your children about online safety empowers them to make informed decisions and navigate the digital world with confidence and caution. Keep the lines of communication open and adapt your discussions as they grow and encounter new online experiences.

CHAPTER 12: PRIVACY AND DATA PROTECTION

Protecting Personal Identifiable Information (PII)

Protecting Personal Identifiable Information (PII) in your home office is crucial to ensure the privacy and security of sensitive data. Here's how you can effectively protect PII:

1. Identify PII:

- Understand what constitutes PII, which includes information like names, addresses, phone numbers, Social Security numbers, email addresses, financial details, and more.

2. Minimize Collection:

- Collect only the necessary PII required for your work and avoid collecting excessive information.

3. Encryption:

- Use encryption for sensitive data both during storage and transmission. This adds an extra layer of protection against unauthorized access.

4. Secure Storage:

- Store physical documents containing PII in a locked cabinet or secure location. Use encrypted digital storage for electronic records.

5. Strong Passwords:

- Use strong, unique passwords for your devices, accounts, and any files or documents containing PII.

6. Multi-Factor Authentication (MFA):

- Enable MFA wherever possible, especially for accounts and systems that store or process PII.

7. Regular Updates:

- Keep your operating system, software applications, and security tools up to date to protect against vulnerabilities.

8. Secure Wi-Fi:

- Use a strong, unique password for your Wi-Fi network and enable WPA3 encryption for better security.

9. Limited Access:

- Restrict access to PII to only those who require it for work purposes. Avoid sharing sensitive data unnecessarily.

10. Secure Disposal:

- Properly dispose of physical documents containing PII through shredding or secure disposal methods.

11. Email Security:

- Be cautious when sharing PII through email. Use encrypted email services or share sensitive information through secure channels.

12. Avoid Public Wi-Fi:

- Avoid transmitting or accessing PII when connected to public Wi-Fi networks, as they can be vulnerable to interception.

13. Screen Locking:

- Set up your devices to automatically lock after a period of inactivity to prevent unauthorized access.

14. Secure Printing:

- If you need to print documents containing PII, ensure the printer is secured, and the printed documents are promptly retrieved.

15. Regular Backups:

- Regularly back up your PII data to secure external storage or encrypted cloud storage to ensure data recovery in case of loss.

16. Privacy Screens:

- Use privacy screens on your devices to prevent unauthorized viewing of sensitive information.

17. Regular Audits:

- Periodically review your data storage and access practices to ensure compliance with privacy regulations.

18. Data Retention:

- Establish a data retention policy and securely delete PII that is no longer needed.

By implementing these measures, you can create a secure environment for handling and protecting Personal Identifiable Information in your home office, reducing the risk of data breaches and privacy violations.

Respecting the Privacy of Others

Respecting the privacy of others in your home office is essential for creating a harmonious and respectful environment, especially when sharing space with family members or roommates. Here's how you can ensure privacy for others:

1. Set Clear Boundaries:

- Establish clear boundaries for your work area to indicate when you're in work mode and available for social interactions.

2. Communicate Your Schedule:

- Let family members or roommates know your work schedule so they can plan their activities around it.

3. Use Headphones:

- If you're on video calls or listening to audio, use headphones to avoid disturbing others and keep your conversations private.

4. Respect Quiet Hours:

- If your family members or roommates have designated quiet hours, make an effort to minimize noise during those times.

5. Privacy Screens:

- Use privacy screens on your devices to prevent unintentional exposure of sensitive information to others.

6. Secure Documents:

- Keep any work-related documents containing sensitive information secure and out of reach of others.

7. Avoid Sharing Screens Unintentionally:

- Be mindful when sharing screens during virtual meetings to prevent accidental exposure of personal or confidential information.

8. Ask Before Sharing:

- Before sharing personal or work-related information, ask your family members or roommates if they're comfortable with it.

9. Lock Devices:

- Lock your devices when you're not using them to prevent others from accessing your work-related content.

10. Educate Family Members:

- Explain the importance of privacy and confidential information to your family members or roommates so they understand why you're taking certain precautions.

11. Designate Work-Free Zones:

- Set up areas where work-related discussions or activities are not allowed to ensure a balance between work and personal interactions.

12. Limit Distractions:

- Minimize disruptions by establishing rules about when it's appropriate to interrupt you during work hours.

13. Keep Personal Devices Private:

- If using shared devices, ensure your accounts and data are secured and private.

14. Close Work Sessions:

- At the end of your workday, close any work-related apps, documents, and communication tools to maintain privacy.

15. Respect Individual Needs:

- Be considerate of others' need for quiet time, personal space, and their work or activities.

16. Regular Communication:

- Maintain an open line of communication with your family members or roommates about your work schedule, needs, and potential conflicts.

Respecting the privacy of others in your home office fosters a cooperative and respectful atmosphere where everyone's needs are considered and accommodated: open communication and a willingness to make compromises go a long way in maintaining a harmonious home environment.

CHAPTER 13: SECURE E-COMMERCE AND ONLINE TRANSACTIONS

Safeguarding Online Payments

Safeguarding online payments in your home office is essential to protect your financial information and prevent unauthorized access. Here are steps you can take to ensure secure online payments:

1. Use Trusted Payment Platforms:

- Use reputable and secure payment platforms when making online transactions. Look for well-known and trusted services.

2. Secure Network Connection:

- Ensure you use a secure Wi-Fi network with strong encryption (WPA3) when making online payments.

3. Strong Passwords:

- Use strong and unique passwords for your online payment accounts. Avoid using the same password across multiple platforms.

4. Two-Factor Authentication (2FA):

- Enable 2FA on your payment accounts whenever possible. This adds an extra layer of security by requiring a second verification step.

5. Monitor Account Activity:

- Regularly review your payment account statements for any unauthorized or suspicious transactions.

6. Keep Software Updated:

- Keep your operating system, browser, and security software up to date to protect against vulnerabilities.

7. Beware of Phishing:

- Be cautious of phishing emails or websites that mimic legitimate payment platforms. Always verify the URL and source before entering payment information.

8. Avoid Public Computers:

- Avoid making online payments from public computers or shared devices, as they may not be secure.

9. Use Secure Websites (HTTPS):

- Only enter payment information on websites with a secure connection (https://) and a padlock icon in the address bar.

10. Secure Payment Information:

- Store your payment information securely. Avoid writing down credit card numbers or sharing them with others.

11. Use Virtual Cards or Payment Wallets:

- Consider using virtual credit cards or payment wallets for online transactions. These provide an extra layer of separation between your actual payment information and online transactions.

12. Check Privacy Settings:

- Review the privacy settings of your payment accounts to control the information you share with third parties.

13. Verify Sellers and Merchants:

- When making online purchases, ensure you're buying from reputable sellers or merchants. Read reviews and check their credentials.

14. Protect Your Device:

- Use security measures like screen locks, biometric authentication, and device encryption to prevent unauthorized access to your device.

15. Keep Personal Information Private:

- Avoid sharing unnecessary personal information during online transactions. Only provide the information required for the transaction.

16. Regularly Review Payment Methods:

- Regularly review and remove outdated or unused payment methods from your accounts.

17. Educate Yourself:

- Stay informed about common online payment scams and techniques used by cybercriminals to avoid falling victim to fraud.

By following these steps, you can significantly enhance the security of your online payment transactions and protect your financial information while working from your home office.

Recognizing E-Commerce Scams and Fraud

Recognizing e-commerce scams and fraud is essential to protect yourself from falling victim to online schemes while working from your home office. Here are signs and tips to help you identify and avoid e-commerce scams:

1. Unrealistic Deals:

- Be cautious of deals that seem too good to be true, such as heavily discounted prices on popular items. Scammers often use enticing offers to lure victims.

2. Suspicious URLs:

- Check the website's URL for misspellings, extra characters, or domains that look slightly different from the official site. Only shop from reputable websites.

3. Poor Website Design:

- Be wary of websites with low-quality design, broken links, and missing contact information.

Legitimate e-commerce sites typically have professional layouts.

4. Lack of Contact Information:

- A trustworthy e-commerce site should provide clear contact information, including a physical address, customer support email, and phone number.

5. Payment Methods:

- Avoid websites that only accept unusual payment methods or ask for payment through wire transfers, prepaid cards, or cryptocurrency.

6. No Secure Connection (HTTPS):

- Always ensure the website has a secure connection (https://) and a padlock icon in the address bar before entering payment information.

7. High-Pressure Tactics:

- Beware websites that pressure you to buy immediately by claiming limited stock or an impending deadline. Legitimate businesses don't use high-pressure tactics.

8. Unsolicited Emails or Texts:

- Don't click on links or download attachments from unsolicited emails or texts, as they could lead to phishing websites or malware.

9. Poor Grammar and Spelling:

- Scam websites often have poor grammar and spelling errors in their content. Professional websites typically maintain good writing standards.

10. No Privacy Policy or Terms of Use:

- A legitimate e-commerce site should have clear privacy policies and terms of use that outline how they handle your data and transactions.

11. No Reviews or Feedback:

- Lack of customer reviews or feedback can be a red flag. Research the website and the product to see if there's any credible information available.

12. Pop-Up Ads or Unsolicited Offers:

- Be cautious of pop-up ads or unsolicited offers that appear while browsing, especially if they ask for personal or financial information.

13. Check Domain Age:

- Scam websites may have recently registered domains. You can use online tools to check the age of a domain.

14. Verify Seller Information:

- If buying from third-party sellers on e-commerce platforms, verify their ratings, reviews, and contact information before purchasing.

15. Trust Your Instincts:

- If something feels off or too good to be true, trust your instincts and take the time to research before making a purchase.

16. Use Reputable Platforms:

- Whenever possible, buy from well-known, established e-commerce platforms with robust buyer protection and dispute resolution mechanisms.

17. Keep Software Updated:

- Ensure your operating system and security software are up to date to prevent malware and phishing attacks.

By staying vigilant, conducting research, and using common sense, you can protect yourself from e-commerce scams and fraud while working from your home office.

Tips for Secure Online Shopping

Secure online shopping is essential to protect your financial information and personal data while making purchases for your home office. Here are tips to ensure safe online shopping:

1. Use Trusted Websites:

- Shop from reputable and well-known e-commerce websites. Avoid unfamiliar or suspicious-looking sites.

2. Secure Connection (HTTPS):

- Ensure the website has a secure connection (https://) and a padlock icon in the address bar before entering payment information.

3. Strong Passwords:

- Create strong and unique passwords for your online shopping accounts. Avoid using the same password for multiple accounts.

4. Two-Factor Authentication (2FA):

- Enable 2FA for your online shopping accounts whenever possible to add an extra layer of security.

5. Guest Checkout:

- If you're not a regular shopper on a website, consider using guest checkout to minimize the information you share.

6. Check Seller Ratings:

- If buying from third-party sellers on e-commerce platforms, check their ratings, reviews, and history before purchasing.

7. Avoid Public Wi-Fi:

- Avoid online purchases using public Wi-Fi networks, as they can be vulnerable to interception.

8. Secure Payment Methods:

- Use secure payment methods, such as credit cards or payment services, that offer buyer protection in case of fraud.

9. Monitor Your Statements:

- Regularly review your credit card or bank statements for unauthorized or suspicious transactions.

10. Keep Software Updated:

- Keep your operating system, browser, and security software up to date to protect against vulnerabilities.

11. Be Cautious of Email Offers:

- Be wary of unsolicited emails offering deals that seem too good to be true. Avoid clicking on links in such emails.

12. Review Privacy Policies:

- Understand how the website handles your data by reviewing their privacy policies and terms of use.

13. Use Strong Wi-Fi:

- When purchasing, use a secure and trusted Wi-Fi network with strong encryption.

14. Clear Cookies and Cache:

- Regularly clear your browser's cookies and cache to prevent tracking and improve privacy.

15. Verify Discounts and Coupons:

- If discount codes or coupons are used, ensure they're from reputable sources. Be cautious of fake offers.

16. Avoid Oversharing:

- Only provide the information required for the purchase. Avoid sharing unnecessary personal details.

17. Check Your Browser:

- Use a modern, up-to-date browser that has built-in security features.

18. Review Return Policies:

- Familiarize yourself with the website's return policies if you need to return or exchange items.

19. Use Virtual Cards or Payment Wallets:

- Consider using virtual credit cards or payment wallets for online transactions to add an extra layer of security.

20. Be Skeptical of Pop-Ups:

- Don't trust pop-up ads or links that appear during your shopping. Always go directly to the official website.

By following these tips, you can enjoy secure online shopping experiences for your home office needs while safeguarding your personal and financial information.

CHAPTER 14: STAYING INFORMED ABOUT CYBERSECURITY THREATS

Following Cybersecurity News and Trends

Staying updated on cybersecurity news and trends is essential for maintaining a secure home office environment. Here's how you can effectively follow cybersecurity news and trends:

1. Subscribe to Reputable Sources:

- Subscribe to cybersecurity-focused websites, blogs, newsletters, and magazines that provide reliable and up-to-date information.

2. Follow Security Organizations:

- Follow reputable cybersecurity organizations and associations on social media platforms to receive the latest trends and news updates.

3. Set Google Alerts:

- Set up Google Alerts for relevant cybersecurity keywords to receive notifications about the latest news and developments.

4. Utilize Social Media:

- Follow cybersecurity experts, industry leaders, and organizations on platforms like Twitter, LinkedIn, and Reddit for real-time updates.

5. Participate in Webinars and Events:

- Attend webinars, virtual conferences, and workshops hosted by cybersecurity experts and organizations to stay informed.

6. Join Online Communities:

- Participate in online forums, discussion groups, and communities focused on cybersecurity to share knowledge and insights.

7. Read Industry Reports:

- Look for industry reports, research papers, and whitepapers from reputable cybersecurity firms and organizations.

8. Watch Video Content:

- Subscribe to YouTube channels and podcasts dedicated to cybersecurity topics to receive audio and visual updates.

9. Stay Updated on Data Breaches:

- Keep an eye on reported data breaches and incidents to understand the latest tactics used by cybercriminals.

10. Government Cybersecurity Agencies:

- Follow your country's government's cybersecurity departments or agencies for insights into national cybersecurity efforts and threats.

11. Check Security Software Updates:

- Regularly check for updates from your antivirus and security software providers, as they often share information about emerging threats.

12. Read Security Blogs:

- Follow blogs by cybersecurity experts and professionals, where they share insights, analyses, and advice.

13. Cybersecurity Podcasts:

- Listen to cybersecurity-focused podcasts during your commute or downtime to stay informed about the latest trends.

14. Explore Online Courses:

- Enroll in online courses related to cybersecurity to deepen your understanding of current threats and solutions.

15. Engage with Experts:

- Engage in conversations with cybersecurity experts on social media platforms to gain insights and clarify doubts.

16. Stay Informed About Regulations:

- Stay updated on any changes in cybersecurity regulations or compliance standards relevant to your work.

17. Join Professional Networks:

- Join professional networks, such as LinkedIn groups or industry forums, where cybersecurity discussions are active.

By consistently engaging with reliable sources of cybersecurity news and trends, you'll be better equipped to adapt your security practices to emerging threats and protect your home office effectively.

Subscribing to Security Alerts and Notifications

Subscribing to security alerts and notifications is an excellent way to stay informed about potential threats and vulnerabilities affecting your home office. Here's how to effectively set up and manage these alerts:

1. Security Software Notifications:

- Ensure that your antivirus, firewall, and other security software are configured to provide real-time notifications about threats and updates.

2. Email Alerts from Reputable Sources:

- Subscribe to email alerts from reputable cybersecurity websites, blogs, and organizations that provide regular updates on the latest threats, vulnerabilities, and best practices.

3. Google Alerts:

- Set up Google Alerts for relevant keywords related to cybersecurity, data breaches, and other security topics. You'll receive email notifications whenever new content matching your keywords is published.

4. Social Media Notifications:

- Follow cybersecurity experts, industry leaders, and organizations on social media platforms like Twitter and LinkedIn. Turn on notifications for their posts to receive real-time updates.

5. Vendor Notifications:

- If you use specific software or services, subscribe to vendor notifications. They often send out alerts about security patches and updates.

6. Threat Intelligence Feeds:

- Some cybersecurity organizations and services offer threat intelligence feeds that provide real-time information about emerging threats. Consider subscribing to these feeds.

7. CERT Notifications:

- Subscribe to notifications from Computer Emergency Response Teams (CERTs) or similar cybersecurity agencies in your country. They provide alerts about significant cyber threats.

8. Industry Newsletters:

- Sign up for newsletters from cybersecurity news websites, which often send summaries of the latest security news and trends.

9. Browser Notifications:

- Some websites offer browser notifications when new content is published. You can enable these notifications for cybersecurity news sites.

10. Podcasts and YouTube Channels:

- Subscribe to cybersecurity podcasts and YouTube channels that cover the latest trends and insights. Many creators also offer notifications when new content is available.

11. Mobile Apps:

- Install mobile apps from cybersecurity news sources and organizations. These apps can send push notifications about breaking news and threats.

12. Security Blogs:

- Subscribe to security blogs from reputable sources that regularly publish articles about recent security incidents, vulnerabilities, and best practices.

13. Threat Intelligence Platforms:

- Consider using threat intelligence platforms that aggregate and deliver information about emerging threats and vulnerabilities directly to your inbox.

14. Forum and Community Notifications:

- If you're part of cybersecurity forums or online communities, enable notifications for important threads or discussions.

15. Government Alerts:

- In some regions, government agencies provide alerts about cybersecurity threats. Subscribe to notifications from these agencies if available.

Remember to manage your notifications effectively to avoid becoming overwhelmed with information. Tailor your subscriptions to your specific needs and preferences, and regularly review the alerts to stay informed about the latest security developments relevant to your home office setup.

Participating in Cybersecurity Communities

Participating in cybersecurity communities is a valuable way to enhance your knowledge, share insights, and stay updated on your home office's latest trends and best practices. Here's how you can effectively engage with cybersecurity communities:

1. Choose Relevant Communities:

- Identify online forums, social media groups, discussion boards, and platforms focusing on cybersecurity topics. Look for communities that align with your interests and expertise.

2. Introduce Yourself:

- When you join a community, introduce yourself and mention your background and interests in cybersecurity. This helps you connect with fellow members.

3. Be Respectful and Professional:

- Maintain a respectful and professional tone in all your interactions. Avoid personal attacks and engage in constructive conversations.

4. Participate Regularly:

- Consistently engage with the community by participating in discussions, asking questions, and sharing your knowledge.

5. Share Insights and Resources:

- Share relevant articles, resources, tools, and insights that you come across. This contributes to the community's knowledge base.

6. Ask Thoughtful Questions:

- Don't hesitate to ask questions if you seek advice or clarification on cybersecurity topics. Ensure your questions are clear and relevant.

7. Offer Help and Solutions:

- If you have expertise in certain areas, assist others needing guidance. Provide solutions and suggestions based on your knowledge.

8. Learn from Others:

- Take advantage of the diverse expertise within the community. Learn from the experiences and insights of other members.

9. Stay Updated:

- Regularly check in to stay updated on the latest discussions, news, and trends. Many communities share real-time information.

10. Respect Confidentiality:

- Avoid sharing sensitive or confidential information about your work or home office setup that could compromise security.

11. Follow Rules and Guidelines:

- Familiarize yourself with the community's rules and guidelines. Adhere to their policies to maintain a positive and collaborative environment.

12. Network and Connect:

- Engage with fellow members, connect with professionals in your field, and build a network to benefit your cybersecurity journey.

13. Attend Virtual Events:

- Many cybersecurity communities organize webinars, virtual conferences, and meetups. Participate in these events to learn from experts and connect with peers.

14. Share Real-World Experiences:

- Share your own experiences, challenges, and successes in cybersecurity. Real-world stories can provide valuable insights to the community.

15. Be Open to Learning:

- The cybersecurity landscape is ever-evolving. Stay open to learning new techniques, tools, and approaches from fellow community members.

16. Respect Differences:

- Cybersecurity communities can have members from diverse backgrounds and perspectives. Be respectful of differing opinions and viewpoints.

By actively participating in cybersecurity communities, you can enhance your knowledge, grow your professional network, and contribute to the broader cybersecurity community while ensuring a secure home office environment.

CHAPTER 15: CONTINUOUS IMPROVEMENT AND EDUCATION

Regularly Assessing Your Cybersecurity Measures

Regularly assessing your cybersecurity measures is crucial for maintaining a secure home office environment. Here's a step-by-step guide to help you effectively assess and enhance your cybersecurity measures:

1. Schedule Assessments:

- Set a schedule for regular cybersecurity assessments, such as quarterly or semi-annually, to ensure consistent monitoring.

2. Review Security Policies:

- Start by reviewing your existing security policies and procedures to ensure they are up to date and aligned with current threats.

3. Identify Assets and Risks:

- Identify your home office's assets (devices, data, software) and assess the potential risks associated with each asset.

4. Vulnerability Assessment:

- Conduct vulnerability assessments using security tools or services to identify any vulnerabilities in your network or systems.

5. Penetration Testing:

- Consider hiring professionals to conduct penetration testing simulating real-world attacks to identify weaknesses.

6. Software Updates:

- Ensure all your software, including operating systems, applications, and security tools, is current.

7. Password Audit:

- Review and update your passwords. Ensure you're using strong and unique passwords for all your accounts.

8. Multi-Factor Authentication (MFA):

- Implement MFA wherever possible to add an extra layer of security to your accounts.

9. Network Security:

- Review your network security measures, including firewalls, router settings, and Wi-Fi security protocols.

10. Device Security:

- Ensure all your devices have security measures, including antivirus software, encryption, and secure passwords.

11. Data Backup:

- Regularly back up your important data to secure external storage or cloud services to prevent data loss.

12. Privacy Settings:

- Review the privacy settings on your devices, software, and online accounts to ensure they're appropriately configured.

13. Email Security:

- Review your email security settings and be cautious of phishing emails and attachments.

14. Secure File Sharing:

- Assess how you share files and collaborate securely. Use encrypted file-sharing tools if needed.

15. Incident Response Plan:

- Review your incident response plan to ensure it's updated and effective in case of a security breach.

16. Training and Education:

- Assess your knowledge and training needs in cybersecurity. Consider taking courses or attending webinars to stay updated.

17. User Access Control:

- Review the access permissions for your accounts and devices. Ensure only necessary users have access.

18. Physical Security:

- Review the physical security measures in your home office, such as locks, security cameras, and visitor access.

19. Remote Access:

- If you access your home office remotely, ensure remote connections are secure and encrypted.

20. Documentation:

- Keep a record of your assessments, findings, and improvements. This will help you track progress and changes over time.

21. Stay Informed:

- Stay updated on the latest cybersecurity threats and trends by following news sources and professional communities.

Regularly assessing your cybersecurity measures and making necessary improvements will help you stay ahead of potential threats and maintain a secure home office environment for your work activities.

Learning from Security Incidents and Mistakes

Learning from security incidents and mistakes in your home office is crucial in enhancing your cybersecurity practices. Here's how you can effectively learn and improve:

1. Incident Review:

- After any security incident or mistake, conduct a thorough review to understand what happened, how it happened, and the impact.

2. Identify Root Causes:

- Dig deep to identify the root causes of the incident or mistake. Was it due to a technical vulnerability, human error, lack of awareness, or other factors?

3. Document Findings:

- Document your findings from the incident review. This documentation will help you avoid similar mistakes in the future.

4. Adjust Security Measures:

- Based on the incident's findings, adjust your security measures, policies, and procedures to prevent similar incidents from occurring again.

5. Update Training and Education:

- If the incident was caused by human error or lack of awareness, consider updating your training and education efforts to address the specific issue.

6. Implement Remediation Steps:

- Put in place specific remediation steps to address the vulnerabilities or weaknesses that led to the incident.

7. Enhance Monitoring:

- Improve your monitoring and detection systems to catch and address potential threats or issues earlier.

8. Communication and Reporting:

- If the incident affected others or external parties, communicate transparently about what happened and the steps taken to resolve it.

9. Share Lessons Learned:

- Share the lessons from the incident with your colleagues, friends, or family members to help them avoid similar mistakes.

10. Conduct Training Workshops:

- Consider conducting training workshops or presentations to raise awareness about the incident and how to prevent it.

11. Stay Updated:

- Stay informed about the latest security trends and cybersecurity incidents to improve your practices continuously.

12. Evaluate Incident Response Plan:

- After an incident, review your incident response plan to ensure it effectively addresses the type of incident you encountered.

13. Test Recovery Procedures:

- If the incident led to data loss or disruptions, test your recovery procedures to ensure you can restore your systems and data.

14. Seek Expert Advice:

- If you're unsure about the best way to address the incident or prevent similar incidents, seek advice from cybersecurity experts.

15. Cultivate a Learning Culture:

- Foster a culture of learning from mistakes and incidents, encouraging open communication and continuous improvement.

16. Regularly Review and Update:

- Periodically review your security measures, incident response plan, and training materials to ensure they remain effective and up to date.

Learning from security incidents and mistakes is an ongoing process that helps you adapt and improve your cybersecurity practices. By taking a proactive approach, you can better protect your home office environment and the sensitive information you handle.

Encouraging a Cybersecurity Culture at Home

Encouraging a cybersecurity culture at home, especially in your home office, is essential to create a secure environment for your work and personal activities. Here's how you can promote a strong cybersecurity culture:

1. Lead by Example:

- Be a role model by consistently practicing good cybersecurity habits yourself.

2. Educate and Raise Awareness:

- Educate your family members or roommates about cybersecurity risks, best practices, and the importance of protecting sensitive information.

3. Establish Clear Guidelines:

- Set clear guidelines for securely using devices, software, and online platforms within your home office space.

4. Regular Training and Workshops:

- Organize regular cybersecurity training sessions or workshops for your household members to enhance their knowledge.

5. Share Real-Life Examples:

- Share real-life examples of cybersecurity incidents or breaches to illustrate the potential consequences of poor security practices.

6. Use Positive Reinforcement:

- Acknowledge and reward family members who consistently follow cybersecurity practices.

7. Create a Secure Environment:

- Implement security measures like strong passwords, antivirus software, and secure Wi-Fi networks in your home office setup.

8. Encourage Privacy Awareness:

- Teach your household members to respect privacy, both their own and others, while using devices and online services.

9. Regularly Update Software:

- Emphasize the importance of updating all devices and software to protect against vulnerabilities.

10. Secure File Sharing:

- Teach safe methods for sharing files and documents and discourage using unsecured platforms.

11. Multi-Factor Authentication (MFA):

- Encourage using MFA for online accounts to add an extra layer of security.

12. Safe Internet Practices:

- Teach safe browsing habits, avoiding suspicious links, and being cautious with downloads.

13. Secure Social Media Usage:

- Highlight the risks of oversharing personal information on social media platforms.

14. Limit Device Access:

- Set guidelines on who can access devices in your home office and under what conditions.

15. Discuss Cyberbullying and Online Etiquette:

- Address cyberbullying and teach good online etiquette to promote respectful behaviour.

16. Report Suspicious Activity:

- Encourage household members to report suspicious emails, messages, or activities.

17. Regular Check-Ins:

- Schedule regular discussions to review cybersecurity practices, share updates, and address concerns.

18. Secure Remote Work Practices:

- If multiple family members work remotely, guide them on secure remote work practices.

19. Use Parental Controls:

- If children use devices in your home office, implement appropriate parental controls and safety measures.

20. Celebrate Cybersecurity Awareness Month:

- October is recognized as Cybersecurity Awareness Month. Use this time to emphasize the importance of cybersecurity.

By fostering a cybersecurity culture at home, you're not only protecting your home office environment but also helping create a safer online experience for everyone in your household. Regular communication, education, and awareness-building efforts will go a long way in ensuring a secure digital lifestyle for your family.

APPENDIX:

Cybersecurity resources and tools

Some useful cybersecurity resources and tools that can help you enhance your knowledge and protect your home office and personal data:

1. **National Cyber Security Centre (NCSC)**: The NCSC provides valuable cybersecurity advice and guidance for individuals and organizations. They offer practical tips, resources, and alerts about the latest threats.

Website: https://www.ncsc.gov.uk/

2. **Cybersecurity and Infrastructure Security Agency (CISA)**: CISA is a U.S. government agency that offers a wealth of cybersecurity resources, including tips, best practices, and alerts for home users.

Website: https://www.cisa.gov/

3. **Electronic Frontier Foundation (EFF)**: EFF is a non-profit organization dedicated to defending civil liberties in the digital world. They provide resources on online privacy, security, and advocacy.

Website: https://www.eff.org/

4. **StaySafeOnline.org**: Managed by the National Cyber Security Alliance (NCSA), this website offers

tips and resources for staying safe online, including free cybersecurity awareness materials.

Website: https://staysafeonline.org/

5. **Have I Been Pwned**: A website that allows you to check if your email address or online accounts have been compromised in data breaches.

Website: https://haveibeenpwned.com/

8. **OpenVPN**: An open-source VPN client and server software that allows you to create secure encrypted connections.

Website: https://openvpn.net/

9. **Wireshark**: A powerful and popular network protocol analyzer that helps you analyze and troubleshoot network traffic for potential security issues.

Website: https://www.wireshark.org/

10. **Tor Browser**: A privacy-focused web browser that routes your internet traffic through the Tor network, providing enhanced anonymity and security.

Website: https://www.torproject.org/

11. **KeePass**: An open-source password manager that lets you securely store and manage your passwords.

Website: https://keepass.info/

12. **Secunia Personal Software Inspector (PSI)**: A tool that scans your computer for outdated software and provides updates to keep your applications secure.

Always verify the legitimacy and security of any software or tools before downloading or installing them. Keeping yourself informed and using reliable cybersecurity resources and tools can significantly enhance online safety and protect your home office environment.

SECURITY CHECKLIST FOR HOME OFFICE

A comprehensive security checklist for your home office to help you create a safe and secure environment for your work and personal activities:

1. **Network Security:**

- ☐ Change the default router login credentials.

- ☐ Enable WPA3 encryption or at least WPA2 with a strong, unique Wi-Fi password.

- ☐ Disable Wi-Fi Protected Setup (WPS) if not needed.

- ☐ Regularly update the router's firmware.

- ☐ Enable firewall protection on the router.

- ☐ Disable remote administration on the router.

2. **Device Security:**

- ☐ Use strong and unique passwords for all devices (computers, smartphones, tablets, etc.).

- ☐ Enable biometric authentication (e.g., fingerprint or facial recognition) on devices.

- ☐ Set up a screen lock on all devices with a time-out feature.

- ☐ Enable full-disk encryption on computers and smartphones.

- ☐ Keep devices updated with the latest operating system and security patches.

- ☐ Install reputable antivirus and anti-malware software on computers.

3. **Data Security:**

- ☐ Regularly back up important data to an external hard drive or secure cloud storage.

- ☐ Use encryption for sensitive files and folders.

- ☐ Limit access to sensitive data by implementing user accounts with appropriate permissions.

- ☐ Physically secure sensitive documents and data in a locked cabinet or drawer.

4. **Internet and Email Practices:**

- ☐ Be cautious about clicking links and downloading attachments from unknown or suspicious sources.

- ☐ Enable two-factor authentication (2FA) for email accounts and other critical services.

- ☐ Use a secure email service that supports encryption.

5. **Physical Security:**

- Lock your home office when not in use.

- Consider installing a security camera or a security system for added protection.

- Keep sensitive documents out of sight when not in use.

6. **Remote Access and VPN:**

- Use a Virtual Private Network (VPN) for secure remote access to your home network.

- Avoid using public Wi-Fi for work-related tasks without using a VPN.

7. **Software Security:**

- Use reputable software from trusted sources and verify app permissions before installation.

- Keep all software, including operating systems, applications, and plugins, updated with the latest patches.

8. **Children and Guest Access:**

- Implement parental controls and appropriate content filtering for devices accessible to children.

- Set up a separate guest network for visitors to your home office.

9. **Video Conferencing and Virtual Meetings:**

- ☐ Use password protection for virtual meetings and webinars.

- ☐ Be cautious about screen sharing and sharing sensitive information during virtual meetings.

10. **Privacy and Data Protection:**

- ☐ Regularly review and update privacy settings on social media and other online accounts.

- ☐ Avoid oversharing personal information online.

11. **Security Awareness and Education:**

- ☐ Stay informed about the latest cybersecurity threats and best practices.

- ☐ Educate family members about cybersecurity risks and safe online practices.

12. **Incident Response Plan:**

- ☐ Create an incident response plan detailing steps to take in case of a security breach or incident.

Remember, cybersecurity is an ongoing process. Regularly review and update your security measures to stay protected against evolving threats.

GLOSSARY OF CYBERSECURITY TERMS

This glossary should provide you with a solid foundation to understand various cybersecurity concepts and terminology commonly used in the field:

Malware: Short for malicious software, malware is any software specifically designed to harm, infiltrate, or exploit computer systems and networks. Common types include viruses, worms, Trojans, and ransomware.

Phishing: A type of cyber attack where attackers send deceptive emails or messages to trick individuals into revealing sensitive information or clicking on malicious links.

Firewall: A security system that monitors and controls incoming and outgoing network traffic based on predefined security rules. It acts as a barrier between a trusted internal network and an untrusted external network (usually the Internet).

Encryption: The process of converting data into a code to prevent unauthorized access. Encrypted data can only be decrypted and read by those with the proper decryption key.

Vulnerability: A weakness or flaw in a system's design, implementation, or configuration that attackers could exploit to gain unauthorized access or compromise the system's security.

Penetration Testing: Also known as ethical hacking or white-hat hacking, it involves simulating cyber attacks on a system or network to identify vulnerabilities and assess security measures.

Zero-Day Vulnerability: A security flaw in software or hardware that is not known to the vendor and for which no patch or fix exists. Attackers can exploit zero days before a solution is developed.

Social Engineering: A method attackers use to manipulate people into revealing sensitive information or performing certain actions, often through psychological manipulation and deception.

Two-Factor Authentication (2FA): A security process that requires users to provide two different forms of identification to access an account or system, such as a password and a one-time verification code sent to a mobile device.

Brute Force Attack: An automated and systematic trial-and-error method used by attackers to guess passwords or encryption keys until they find the correct one.

Denial-of-Service (DoS) Attack: An attack that aims to make a computer system or network unavailable to its users by overwhelming it with a high volume of traffic or resource requests.

Internet of Things (IoT): A network of physical devices, vehicles, appliances, and other objects embedded with sensors, software, and connectivity that enables them to collect and exchange data.

Patch: A piece of software designed to update or fix issues in a computer program or operating system to improve security or add new features.

Man-in-the-Middle (MitM) Attack: A type of attack where a cybercriminal intercepts and relays communications between two parties without their knowledge, potentially eavesdropping or altering the data.

Data Breach: Unauthorized access, disclosure, or exposure of sensitive or confidential data.

Digital Forensics: The process of collecting, analyzing, and preserving electronic evidence to investigate cybercrimes or security incidents.

Ransomware: A type of malware that encrypts a victim's data and demands a ransom payment for the decryption key.

Antivirus Software: Software designed to detect, prevent, and remove malware from a computer or network.

Virtual Private Network (VPN): A secure and encrypted network connection that allows users to access the internet or connect to a private network remotely.

Patch Management: The process of acquiring, testing, and deploying patches and updates to software applications and operating systems to keep them secure and up to date.

CONCLUSION

- Emphasizing the Importance of Cybersecurity at Home

- Encouraging Ongoing Learning and Adaptation

- Empowering Readers to Create a Safe and Secure Home Office Environment

ABOUT THE AUTHOR

Gregory Dharma LePard has been active in Information Technology and Cybersecurity for over 20 years. He is an innovative and driven professional with a culmination of experience in Cybersecurity, Sales Engineering, Account Management and Ethical Hacking. With his passion for cybersecurity and the ever-evolving cybersecurity landscape, Gregory is always on the hunt for knowledge, and it shows he is continually getting certifications related to the cybersecurity field, giving him a wide breadth of knowledge, and he likes to share it!

Gregory is the co-founder and Chief Evangelist of Cybersnap - a cybersecurity consulting firm providing services from Cybersecurity Training, vCISO, and Cloud to Technical and Security Overviews and Ethical Hacking.

The philosophy of Cybersnap is that we want to bring the human element back to cybersecurity as the first line of defence.

Gregory lives in Canada with his spouse and fur baby.

ACKNOWLEDGEMENTS

"I must start by thanking Imogen Fannon. From reading early drafts to editing, suggesting cover and title options, and designing the layout, she was as important to this book's completion as I was.

I would also like to thank my family for their unwavering support and cheerleading, enabling me to take the leap and follow my dreams.

Thank you so much."

OUR OTHER PUBLICATIONS:

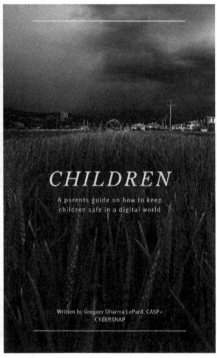

AVAILABLE ON AMAZON

www.ingramcontent.com/pod-product-compliance
Lightning Source LLC
LaVergne TN
LVHW051735050326
832903LV00023B/920